American Culture
Viewing, Listening and Speaking

U0454078

美国文化
视听说

刘秀梅　王振英
陈　曼　冯新平　编著

知识产权出版社
全国百佳图书出版单位

图书在版编目（CIP）数据

美国文化视听说：中文、英文/刘秀梅等编著. —北京：知识产权出版社，2019.1
ISBN 978 - 7 - 5130 - 5638 - 0

Ⅰ.①美… Ⅱ.①刘… Ⅲ.①英语—听说教学—高等学校—教材
Ⅳ.①H319. 39

中国版本图书馆 CIP 数据核字（2018）第 134287 号

内容提要

本书共 10 个单元，涵盖了价值观念、教育体系、家庭结构、社会福利、职业道德及文化冲突与融合等内容。每个单元安排了四部分内容：文化背景介绍、电影简介、听说训练和课后实践项目。

本书旨在让学生形象深入地了解美国文化的同时，通过加强听、说练习全面提升学生的语言综合运用能力，适用于非英语专业高年级本科生和研究生的英语拓展课程。

责任编辑：陈晶晶　　　　　　　　　　责任校对：谷　洋
封面设计：李志伟　　　　　　　　　　责任印制：刘译文

美国文化视听说

刘秀梅　王振英　陈　曼　冯新平　编著

出版发行：**知识产权出版社** 有限责任公司　　　网　　址：http://www.ipph.cn
社　　址：北京市海淀区气象路 50 号院　　　　　邮　　编：100081
责编电话：010 - 82000860 转 8391　　　　　　　责编邮箱：shiny-chjj@163.com
发行电话：010 - 82000860 转 8101/8102　　　　 发行传真：010 - 82000893/82005070/82000270
印　　刷：北京嘉恒彩色印刷有限责任公司　　　 经　　销：各大网上书店、新华书店及相关专业书店
开　　本：720mm×1000mm　1/16　　　　　　　 印　　张：12
版　　次：2019 年 1 月第 1 版　　　　　　　　　 印　　次：2019 年 1 月第 1 次印刷
字　　数：200 千字　　　　　　　　　　　　　　 定　　价：49.00 元
ISBN 978 - 7 - 5130 - 5638 - 0

PREFACE

Language and culture are undeniably intertwined. Language is a reflection of culture. The way we think and view the world is determined by the language we use. Understanding the target culture is not only the means but also the end for English learners in Chinese context.

To know what is on at the cinema is to know what is happening in the United States. Movies are reflections of the real life. They mirror different aspects of American society, including Americans' religious belief, value system and their behavior patterns. Seeing movies is a quick and lively way to understand American society. It's also an efficient way to improve English learners' listening and speaking ability.

The book chooses ten cultural topics which are of the

young language learners' concern. Users of this book can have a profound understanding of the USA through the cultural introduction and the films provided in each chapter. The big and serious topics such as politics, economics and the judicial system are not included in this book.

The target readers of this book include college students and those who are curious for American culture. Each chapter is divided into four parts: cultural foods, movie introduction, listening & speaking activities and movie review & projects. The book can be used as a teaching material for college electives as well as a self-learning material.

January, 2019

Contents

Chapter I   Religious Belief ·· 1

    Part I   Cultural Foods ·· 1

    Part II   *The Ten Commandments* ································· 6

    Part III Listening and Speaking Activities ··················· 8

    Part IV   Movie Review and Projects ························· 14

Chapter II   Wars and the USA ································· 20

    Part I   Cultural Foods ···································· 20

    Part II   *Saving Private Ryan* ··························· 24

    Part III Listening and Speaking Activities ··············· 26

    Part IV   Movie Review and Projects ······················ 31

Chapter III Values and Assumptions ····················· 37

    Part I   Cultural Foods ······························· 37

Part Ⅱ *The Shawshank Redemption* ·················· 43

Part Ⅲ Listening and Speaking Activities ················ 45

Part Ⅳ Movie Review and Projects ·················· 49

Chapter Ⅳ Education ·················· 53

Part Ⅰ Cultural Foods ·················· 53

Part Ⅱ *The Dead Poets Society* ·················· 59

Part Ⅲ Listening and Speaking Activities ················ 61

Part Ⅳ Movie Review and Projects ·················· 68

Chapter Ⅴ Family ·················· 73

Part Ⅰ Cultural Foods ·················· 73

Part Ⅱ *American Beauty* ·················· 82

Part Ⅲ Listening and Speaking Activities ················ 83

Part Ⅳ Movie Review and Projects ·················· 88

Chapter Ⅵ Work Ethics ·················· 93

Part Ⅰ Cultural Foods ·················· 93

Part Ⅱ *The Devil Wears Prada* ·················· 98

Part Ⅲ Listening and Speaking Activities ················ 100

Part Ⅳ   Movie Review and Projects   ·················· 105

Chapter Ⅶ   Welfare System ······························ 110

Part Ⅰ   Cultural Foods ···································· 110

Part Ⅱ   *The Pursuit of Happyness* ·················· 114

Part Ⅲ   Listening and Speaking Activities ·········· 115

Part Ⅳ   Movie Review and Projects   ·················· 120

Chapter Ⅷ   Mass Media ······························· 126

Part Ⅰ   Cultural Foods ···································· 126

Part Ⅱ   *The Truman Show* ························· 131

Part Ⅲ   Listening and Speaking Activities ·········· 132

Part Ⅳ   Movie Review and Projects   ·················· 136

Chapter Ⅸ   Popular Culture ······················ 140

Part Ⅰ   Cultural Foods ···································· 140

Part Ⅱ   *High School Musical* ···················· 147

Part Ⅲ   Listening and Speaking Activities ·········· 148

Part Ⅳ   Movie Review and Projects   ·················· 155

Chapter X   Conflicts and Integration ························· 161

Part Ⅰ   Cultural Foods ······························ 161

Part Ⅱ   *Crash* ······························ 165

Part Ⅲ   Listening and Speaking Activities ··············· 167

Part Ⅳ   Movie Review and Projects ··················· 172

References ································· 177

Chapter Ⅰ   Religious Belief

Introduction to the Chapter

Religion in the United States is characterized by a popularity and diversity of beliefs and practices. Religion influenced and influences the USA in many aspects, such as American politics, education, value system and customs. A majority of Americans report that religion plays a very important role in their lives.

Part Ⅰ   Cultural Foods

Popularity and Diversity of American Religion

Americans are mostly descendants of European immigrants of the 17th and 18th century, as well as immigrants of Latin America, Africa and Asia. America being famous as an "ethnic melting pot" and "religiously United Nations", multiculture nourishes the multi-religious culture. Christianity, Islam, Judaism and Buddhism coexist in this land, with protestantism holding the dominant position. Religion played a vital role in the establishment of the American colonies, the early American life and politics and the founding of the

United States of America.

In the mainstream of American culture, the consciousness that American is different from other countries in the world is ingrained. Many Americans believe that the United States is a special country the God has chosen, and that "the promised land" bears a special responsibility and destiny for the development of all human. They believe USA has the mission to save the entire world from the "Misery", which is the main symbol that distinguishes the United States from other countries.

The ***Bible*** is the holy book of Christianity. More than 40 men, who were moved by the Holy Spirit of God, wrote the books. The *Bible* is a collection of 66 books, according to the protestant, among which 39 books are the Old Testament and 27 books are the New Testament. It covers the story from 1400 BC to 100 AD.

The Old Testament, written in Hebrew language, is the first part of the *Bible*. Christians traditionally divide the Old Testament into four sections: (1) the first five books or Pentateuch (Torah); (2) the history books telling the history of the Israelites, from their conquest of Canaan to their defeat and exile in Babylon; (3) the poetic and "Wisdom books" in various forms, dealing with questions of good and evil in the world; and (4) the books of the biblical prophets, warning of the consequences of turning away from God.

The New Testament, written in Greek, is the second part of the Christian biblical canon. It discusses the teachings and person of Jesus. The New Testament consists of 4 parts: (1) four narratives of the life, teaching, death and resurrection of Jesus called "gospel" or the good news; (2) a narrative of the Apostle ministries in the early church, called the "Acts of the Apostles", and probably written by the same writer as the Gospel of Luke, which it continues; (3) twenty-one letters, often called "epistles" from Greek "epistle", written by various authors, and consisting of Christian doctrine, counsel, instruction, and conflict resolution; and (4) an Apocalypse, the Book of Revelation, which is a book of prophecy, containing some instructions to seven local congregations of Asia Minor, but mostly containing prophetical symbology, about the end times.

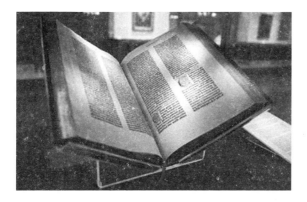

The Influence of the Bible on the English Language

The *Bible*, which is also known as "Book of the books", together with Shakespeare's works is the most influential to English literature and language. When the Bible was translated into the common tongue of the English people, many bible words, phrases, expressions and references quickly became assimilated into the English language and are still in use today.

Some Examples:

Armageddon—Rev 16:16

a doubting Thomas—John 20:27

a (painted) Jezebel—Kings 9:30–37, Rev 2:20

a Judas (goat)—Luke 6:16

a leopard can't change its spots—Jer 13:23

a little bird told me—Eccl 10:20

eat, drink and be merry—Luke 12:19

going the extra mile—Matt 5:41

money is the root of all evil—Tim 6:10

old wives' tales—Tim 4:7

pride goes before a fall—Prov 16:18

practice what you preach—Matt 23:2–3

returning like the prodigal son—Luke 15:11–24

red sky at night, shepherd's delight; red sky in the morning, shepherd's warning—Matt 16:1–3

scapegoat—Lev 16:9–10

seek and you shall find—Matt 7:7

spare the rod, spoil the child—Prov 13:24

the sweat of your brow—Gen 3:17,19

the apple of my eye—Psalm 17:8

the salt of the earth—Matt 5:13

the sun shines on the righteous—Matt 5:45

there's a time and place for everything—Eccl 3:1

the blind leading the blind—Matt 15:14

the writing's on the wall—Dan 5:5−6

their left hand doesn't know what their right hand is doing—Matt 5:3−4

to escape by the skin of your teeth—Job 19:19−20

wolf in sheep's clothing—Matt 7:15

Part II *The Ten Commandments*

The Ten Commandments is a biblical **epic** film made in 1956, produced and directed by Cecil B. DeMille.

The movie draws on the Bible and numerous other sources to **depict** the life of Moses, from his **humble** birth and abandonment in the bull rushes, to his young manhood as a member of the Egyptian ruling class.

When Moses discovers his humble origins, he readjusts his life and ambitions to become an instrument of the Hebrew God and begins a long struggle to free his people from their slavery under the Egyptians. He finally **ascends** Mount Sinai and is given the Ten Commandments by God. Along the way he performs some useful miracles like parting the Red Sea, turning the Nile into a river of blood, and changing his **staff** into a snake.

New Words and Phrases:

epic	n.	史诗
depict	v.	描述;描画
humble	adj.	谦逊的;卑微的
ascend	v.	攀登;上升
staff	n.	职员;参谋;棒;支撑

Part III   Listening and Speaking Activities

Task 1: View and listen to the Clip: *Birth of Moses*, and fill in the blanks.

Memnet: What have you found?

Bithiah: The answer to my prayers.

Memnet: You prayed for a basket?

Bithiah: No. I prayed for a son.

Memnet: Your husband is _____ dead.

Bithiah: And he has asked the Nile god to bring me this beautiful boy.

Memnet: Do you know the pattern of this cloth?

Bithiah: If my son is covered in it...it is a **royal** robe.

Memnet: Royal? It is the Levite cloth of a Hebrew slave. This child was put upon the water to _____ your father's **edict**.

Bithiah: I am the Pharaoh's daughter, and this is my son. He shall be **reared** in my house as the Prince of the Two Lands.

Memnet: My mother and her mother before her _____ the Pharaoh's service. I will not see you make this son of slaves a prince of Egypt.

Bithiah: You will see it, Memnet. You will see him walk with his head among the eagles. And you will serve him as you serve me.

Fill the ark with water. _____ silence.

Raise your hands, Memnet. What you have buried in the Nile shall remain buried in your heart. _____.

Memnet: I will be silent.

Bithiah: The day you break that oath will be the last your eyes shall ever see. You will be the glory of Egypt, my son. Mighty in words and deeds. Kings shall bow before you. Your name will live when the **pyramids** are dust. And... because I drew you from the water, you shall be called Moses.

New Words and Phrases:

royal   adj.   皇家的

edict   n.   法令;布告

rear   v.   培养;树立;栽种

pyramid   n.   金字塔

Notes:

Moses ben Amram, who is formerly known as Prince Moses, was crown prince of Upper and Lower Egypt, shepherd of Midian. He ultimately became the Hebrew leader and law giver notable for delivering his people out of their bondage in Egypt to Mount Sinai, where he received the Ten Commandments from God upon the mountain's summit. Before escaping to Midian, he was a crown prince of Egypt and the favor of Pharaoh Sethi Ⅰ. When he knew his true heritage, which was kept from him by his adoptive mother Bithiah, he refused to be called the son of Pharaoh's daughter and saw the affliction of his people in slavery. In order to save Joshua from Baka, an Egyptian master-builder, Moses murdered him. When Rameses Ⅱ learned this from Dathan, he brought Moses unto the shadow of Sethi's justice, who ordered him to be exiled from Egypt. Moses took refuge in Midian, and in the house of Jethro the sheikh of Midian, he became the shepherd of Jethro's flocks. After some time, Moses was attracted by the burning bush, onto which God ordered him to go back to Egypt and deliver the Hebrews away from bondage.

Task 2: Watch the Clip: *Dathan and Remeses' Deal*, work in group of two to do the following exercises.

1. Share notes with your partner.

2. Discuss the reasons behind Dathan and Remeses' deal.

From Remeses' perspective:

From Dathan's perspective:

3. Role play Dathan and Remeses with your partner.

New Words and Phrases：

deliverer	n.	拯救者
haggle	v.	讨价还价
scepter	n.	节杖(象征君权)；王权
blade	n.	刀锋

Notes：

Dathan was a chief Hebrew-overseer, and later Governor of Goshen as appointed by Rameses Ⅱ before his reign. When as a slave, he was a confidant and assistant of Baka, Pharaoh Sethi Ⅰ's master builder. After Baka's death, Dathan overhears Joshua, who firmly believes that Moses is the deliverer.

Task 3： Listen to the Clip：*Sephora's Expression of Love*, and complete the sentences.

A jewel has brilliant fire, but _____.

Our hands are not so soft, but _____.

Our bodies not so white, but _____.

Our lips are not **perfumed**...but _____.

Love is not an art to us. _____.

We are not dressed in gold and fine **linen**. _____.

Our tents are not the **columned** halls of Egypt,

but _____.

We can offer you little...but _____.

New Words and Phrases：

perfume	v.	洒香水于……；使……带香味

| linen | n. | 亚麻布;亚麻制品 |
| column | n. | 列;专栏;圆柱,柱形物 |

Notes:

Sephora was a shepherd girl in Midian and the eldest daughter of Jethro, the sheik of Midian. Sephora was the second wife of Moses, and the mother of Gershom. She was also a fervent believer of the God of Abraham.

"Your eyes are sharp as they are beautiful!"—Moses to Sephora

Task 4: Watch the Clip: *the Ten Plagues by Moses*, work in groups to finish the two tasks.

1. Relay the story of the Ten Plagues, one plague by one person each time.

2. Have the character analysis of Moses, Remeses, Sephora and Nefretiri. The following words are for your reference.

arrogant	aggressive	unconventional	rebellious	selfless
rough	dogmatic	reserved	passionate	finicky
insightful	nitpicking	pleasant	repulsive	prudent
generous	mild-tempered	sincere	decent	manful
graceful	liberal	critical	sensible	open-minded
gentle	tolerant	fussy	stubborn	tricky

Task 5: Reflect on memorable sentences. Which sentences are still in your mind? Which sentence impresses you most? Why? Share your understanding of the sentences with your friends. Some sentences are listed below for your reference.

1. God made men. Men made slaves.

2. Ambition knows no father.

3. There is a beauty beyond the senses, Nefretiri. Beauty like the quiet green valleys and still waters. Beauty of the spirit that you cannot understand.

4. Your tongue will dig your grave.

Part IV   Movie Review and Projects

The Ten Commandments

Cecil B. DeMille's *The Ten Commandments* is, in many ways, the summit of screen achievement. It is not just a great and powerful motion picture, although it is that; it is also a new human experience. If there were but one print of this Paramount picture, the place of its showing would be the focus of a world-wide **pilgrimage**. As it is, Cecil B. DeMille's **lofty** and crowning achievement will bring into theatres throughout the world the most important segment of potential audiences: the people who do not attend movies regularly or do not go at all. They will go to this one. *The Ten Commandments* cannot be evaluated by ordinary critical standards. It establishes its own measure of evaluation in almost every way, speaking theatrically, and it cannot even be judged on that basis alone, since it is also a profound and important spiritual message.

"Proclaim liberty throughout the lands, unto all the inhabitants thereof." So says Moses to the Jews as the Chosen People approach the River Jordan and Moses leaves them. This is the theme of this great picture, liberty under God, the sanctity of the individual and his struggle for freedom from oppression created **tyrannical** state and the men who see no higher authority than that with which they invest themselves. The story, in its bare outlines, is familiar to everyone. Moses, born to a Hebrew family in slavery in Egypt, is spared by his mother from the death **decreed** by the Pharaoh when she puts the infant in a basket and sets it adrift on the Nile. The child is found by the Pharaoh's daughter and raised as her own child, as a prince of Egypt. There comes a time when Moses learns he is Hebrew, not Egyptian, and when he must choose which future he will accept. Having chosen his own people, he then leads the Jews out of Egypt and, after years of hardship and wandering, delivers them to the Promised Land.

DeMille has augmented the Bible story with careful research, wisely careful that the story as he presented it will not give offense to any believers, Christian, Jew or Mohammedan. It stresses our common brotherhood, as children of Abraham, rather than the differences which the years have brought.

Charlton Heston as Moses is splendid, handsome and princely (and human) in the scenes dealing with him as a young man, and majestic and terrible as his role demands it. He is the great Michelangelo conception of Moses but rather as the inspiration for the sculptor might have been than as a derivation. Yul Brynner is magnificent as Rameses Ⅱ , an intelligent and not entirely cruel king but one caught in a cataclysmic moment of history. They make a fine counterpoint, Heston and Brynner. Anne Baxter is very good as the Egyptian princess who wants Heston but gets Brynner, an intelligent woman for her time but only dimly aware of the forces at work that defeat her purposes. Edward G. Robinson plays Dathan, the **turncoat** Hebrew who tries to persuade the Jews that while their chains are oppressive they still represent a kind of security and that freedom is a potentially risky thing. Yvonne De Carlo is very fine as the simple Sephora, whom Moses took to wife and who bore him his son. Debra Paget is lovely and **pathetic** as Lilia, possessed by Dathan but loving John Derek, who makes a good Joshua. Nina Foch is excellent as Bithiah, the Egyptian princess who reared Moses; Cedric Hardwicke is very fine, especially so, as the Pharaoh Sethi, a kind of Egyptian Louis XIV. Judith Anderson has **menace** and power as the slave Memnet, and Martha Scott is very effective as Yochabel, Moses' true mother. Vincent Price, John Carradine, Henry Wilcoxon, Douglass Dumbrille, Oliver Deering, Donald Curtis, H. B. Warner, Frank DeKova, Eduard Franz, Lawrence Dobkin, Julia Faye and Ian Keith are among the others in the huge cast who have especially important characters and who make contributions to the picture.

There is so much about *The Ten Commandments* that crics for comment, for appreciation and for approval that it is simply impossible to relay it all here. DeMille himself introduces the picture with a modest and engaging appearance. He also supplies a running

commentary that is **discreet** and yet helpful. To sum up, *The Ten Commandments was a dream in the mind of Cecil B. DeMille beyond* what anyone else had ever projected, and he has brought it off. It is, in that misused but here accurate word, unique. There is no other picture like it. There will be none. If it could be summed up in a word, the word would be **sublime**. And the man responsible for that, when all is said and done is Cecil B. DeMille. ❶

New Words and Phrases:

pilgrimage	n.	朝圣之行
lofty	adj.	崇高的
tyrannical	adj.	残暴的;专横的
decree	v.	颁布法令
turncoat	n.	变节者;叛变者
pathetic	adj.	可怜的;悲哀的
menace	n.	威胁;恐吓
commentary	n.	评论;注释
discreet	adj.	谨慎的
sublime	adj.	庄严的;令人崇敬的

Project 1: Read the Movie Review again. Please locate the words and sentences to show the author's comment on the movie. Then brainstorm the sentences to show your general comments on a movie of your free choice. Examples are provided for your references.

---

❶ The Ten Commandments [EB/OL]. (2014 – 07 – 12) [2017 – 12 – 05]. https://www. hollywoodreporter. com/news.

the summit of screen achievement, lofty and crowning...

_____

_____

_____

_____

Great Movie	1. The movie is worth repeated viewing. 2. *Blue Ruin* is far too addictive to give up until the bitter end. 3. _____ . 4. _____ . 5. _____ .
Bad Movie	1. You're better off saving your time, your money, and popcorn. 2. *Forest Gump*, much like the "box of chocolates", has a couple of good little shots. But most of the scenes, too sweet by half, should be in the trash. 3. _____ . 4. _____ 5. _____
Okay Movie	1. *Boyhood* may not be a great movie. But the power the film find in the beauty of passing time, which attracts anyone interested in the art of film. 2. _____ . 3. _____ . 4. _____ .

Project 2: Have a comparison between Tang Xuanzang in *Journey to the West* and Moses in *the Ten Commandments*. What differences and similarities can you find? You are supposed to give 1 ~ 2 examples to illustrate your points.

	Tang Xuanzang	**Moses**
Early life experience		
Youth life experience		
Pains in *Journey to the West & Exodus*		
Gains in *Journey to the West & Exodus*		
Legacy to the people		

Chapter II Wars and the USA

Introduction to this Chapter

Young as it is, the United States has undergone a number of severe conflicts and bloody wars. Win or lose, every warfare that the United States was involved in, from the Civil War to the Vietnam War, has marked an outset of a new era in its history. However, war is costly in life and wealth, just as Ernest Hemingway once remarked, "In modern war, there is nothing neither sweet nor fitting in your dying. You will die like a dog for no good reason."

Part I Cultural Foods

American Civil War

The Civil War began in 1861. Fearing that the slavery system was in peril after the election of an anti-slavery U.S. president Abraham Lincoln, eleven states with slavery in the southern United States declared their separation from the country and formed the Confederate States, also known as "the Confederacy", and then initiated the Civil War. The northern part, also known as "the Union", led by Republican

Abraham Lincoln, consisted of every slave-free U. S. state as well as five slave-holding states, known as "border states". In 1865, the war ended when the Confederacy surrendered, and slavery was abolished in the United States. As America's bloodiest clash and conflict within its territory, the Civil War resulted in the death of more than 620,000, with millions more injured.

Abraham Lincoln, a strong opponent of slavery, was elected the 16th president of the United States in 1860, just before the outburst of the Civil War. Lincoln was a tactful military strategist and an admired leader: The *Emancipation Proclamation* he issued paved the way for slavery's abolition, while his *Gettysburg Address* stands as one  of the most famous speeches in American history. In April 1865, with the Union on the verge of victory, Abraham Lincoln was assassinated;

his untimely death made him a martyr to the cause of liberty, and now he is widely regarded as one of the greatest presidents in the U. S. history.

World War II

Japanese attack on the American naval fleet at Pearl Harbor in 1941 forced the U. S. into World War II (1939—1945). As a consequence, the country was dramatically altered: food, gas and clothing were restricted; approximately 350,000 American women joined the military during World War II as nurses, drove trucks, repaired airplanes, and performed clerical work to free up men for combat; Japanese Americans were deprived their rights as citizens; people in the U. S. became increasingly reliant on radio reports for news of the fighting overseas; while popular entertainment served to demonize the nation's enemies, it was also regarded as an escapist outlet that allowed Americans brief relief from war worries.

In addition, the U. S. conducted the first and only dropping of the atomic bomb in the world on Japan, which marked the end of World War II. On August 6, 1945, an American B – 29 bomber dropped the world's first atomic bomb over the Japanese city of Hiroshima. The explosion destroyed 90 percent of the city and immediately killed 80,000 people; tens of thousands more would later die of radiation exposure. Three days later, a second B – 29 dropped another A-bomb on Nagasaki, killing an estimated 40,000 people. Japan's Emperor announced his country's unconditional surrender in a radio address on August 15, referring to the devastating power of "a new and most cruel bomb".

The Vietnam War

Over 25 years (1950—1975), the United States battled North Vietnam and its allies in the long, costly and divisive conflict in American history. The conflict was fueled by the ongoing Cold War between the United States and the Soviet Union. The Vietnam War resulted in more than 3 million people (including over 58,000 Americans) killed, and more than half of the dead are Vietnamese civilians. In 1973, President Richard Nixon ordered the withdrawal of U. S. forces; shortly afterwards, communist forces seized control of South Vietnam in 1975, and the country was unified as the Socialist Republic of Vietnam in 1976.

The Vietnam War had a tremendous impact on American society and culture, largely because it was the first American war to be televised. The photographs, videos, and opinions of American journalists, together with the fact that young Americans were dying on foreign soil against an enemy that did not threaten the United States directly, turned much of the American public against the war. This enormous power of the media and public distrust of the government have been a mainstay of American society ever since.

Part Ⅱ   *Saving Private Ryan*

Saving Private Ryan features the story of several World War Ⅱ soldiers who are on a quest to find one man who is fighting somewhere else in Europe. This man, Private James Francis Ryan, has three brothers who were all killed at various places all over the world as American soldiers. This case is brought to the attention of General George Marshall and he ordered Captain John Miller to lead a **squad** of men with the primary task of finding Private Ryan. The squad grows in friendship purely because of the circumstances that allow them enough time together. When they finally find Private James Ryan, Ryan is shocked by the news that all three of his brothers were dead. However, he refuses to return home with Miller and his crew. He is loyal to his fellow soldiers. Miller, though **infuriated**, stays with Ryan and the whole crew takes up arms against the **impending** arrival of German tanks who will attempt to capture a bridge. The Germans arrive and even though the Americans successfully prevent the take-over of the bridge, a number of the men in the squad die. Captain Miller is shot in defense of the bridge and dies too. In the end, the movie takes the audience back to the present-day and the older veteran who turns out to be Private Ryan stands in front of Miller's grave and pays tribute to him.

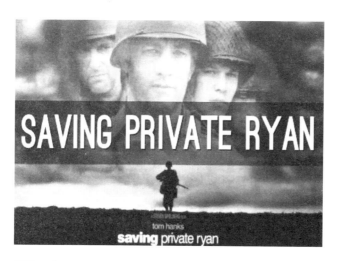

New Words and Phrases：

feature	v.	描述
squad	n.	队
infuriated	adj.	激怒的；十分生气的
impending	adj.	即将发生的；迫在眉睫的

Part III　Listening and Speaking Activities

Task 1: View and listen to the following clip: *Eight to One*, and fill in the blanks with the missing words and expressions.

Jackson: Sir... I have an opinion on this matter.

Miller: Well, by all means, share it with the squad.

Jackson: Well, from my way of thinking, sir, this entire _____ is a serious **misallocation** of valuable military _____.

Miller: Yeah, Go on.

Jackson: Well, it seems to me, Sir, that God gave me a special **gift**, made me a fine _____ of warfare.

Miller: Reiben, pay attention. Now, this is the way to gripe. Continue, Jackson.

Jackson: Well, what I mean by that, Sir, is if you was to put me and this sniper rifle anywhere up to and including one mile of Adolf Hitler with a clear line of sight, sir—Pack your bags, fellas. War's over. Amen.

Reiben: Oh, _____ bumpkin. Hey, so Captain, what about you? I mean,...you don't **gripe** at all?

Miller: I don't gripe to you, Reiben. I'm a captain. There's a chain of _____. Gripes go up, not down. Always up. You gripe to me, I gripe to my _____, so on, so on and so on. I don't gripe to you. I don't gripe in front of you. You should know that as a ranger.

Reiben: I'm sorry, Sir, but, uh... But let's say that you weren't a captain, or that I was a major, what would you say?

Miller: In that case, I'd say, "this is an excellent mission, Sir, with an extremely valuable _____, sir, worthy of my best efforts, Sir. Moreover, I feel heartfelt _____ for the mother of Private James Ryan and I'm more than willing to **lay down** my life, and the lives of my men, especially you, Reiben, to _____ her suffering.

Mellish: He's good.

Caparzo: _____.

New Words and Phrases:

misallocation	n.	错配
gift	n.	天赋;才能
gripe	v.	抱怨;怨言;牢骚
lay down	v phr.	放下

Notes

Adolf Hitler, the leader of Nazi Germany from 1934 to 1945, initiated fascist policies that triggered World War II and led to the deaths of at least 11 million people, including the mass murder of an estimated 6 million Jews.

Task 2: View and listen to the following clip: *George C Marshall's Letter to Mrs. Ryan*, and answer the following questions.

1. Where is Private James Ryan now?

_____

2. How did James do his duty in combat?

_____

3. What is Abraham Lincoln's remark?

_____

New Words and Phrases：

steadfast	adj.	坚定的;不动摇的
campaign	n.	战役;运动
tyranny	n.	暴虐;苛政
compensate	v.	补偿;弥补
sustain	v.	支持;支撑
assuage	v.	缓和;平息
bereavement	n.	丧失亲人

Notes

George Marshall served as Chief of Staff of the United States Army under presidents Franklin D. Roosevelt during World War II. He was praised as the "organizer of victory" by Winston Churchill for his leadership of the Allied victory. After the war, in his service as Secretary of State, Marshall advocated a significant U. S. economic and political commitment to post-war European recovery, the Marshall Plan that bore his name. In recognition of his effort, he was awarded the Nobel Peace Prize in 1953.

Task 3：Watch the Clip：*Captain John Miller's Address on*

Mission to Save Private Ryan, and work in group of two to

1. Share notes with your partner.

2. Discuss the reasons behind their argument.

3. Share with your partner your understanding of Miller's words, "*every man I kill, the farther away from home I feel.*"

Task 4: Listen to the speech: *Blood*, *Toil*, *Tears and Sweat*, and work in group of two to

1. Discuss the main idea and purposes of this speech.

2. Perform the following part of the speech.

We have before us an ordeal of the most grievous kind. We have before us many, many long months of struggle and of suffering. You ask, what is our policy? I can say: It is to wage war, by sea, land and air, with all our might and with all the strength that God can give us; to wage war against a monstrous tyranny, never surpassed in the dark, lamentable catalogue of human crime. That is our policy. You ask, what is our aim? I can answer in one word: It is victory, victory at all costs, victory in spite of all terror, victory, however long and hard the road may be; for without victory, there is no survival. Let that be realized; no survival for the British Empire, no survival for all that the British Empire has stood for, no survival for the urge and impulse of the ages, that mankind will move forward towards its goal. But I take up my task with buoyancy and hope. I feel sure that our cause will not be suffered to fail among men. At this time I feel entitled to claim the aid of all, and I say, "come then, let us go forward together with our united strength. "

Task 5: Reflect on memorable sentences. Which sentences are still in your mind? Which sentence impresses you most? Why? Share your understanding of the sentences with your friends. Some sentences are listed below for your reference.

1. Sometimes I wonder if I've changed so much, my wife is even gonna recognize me whenever it is I get back to her, and how I'll ever be able to, tell about days like today. Ahh, Ryan. I don't know anything about Ryan, I don't care. The man means nothing to me; he's just a name. But if, you know, if going to Ramelle, and finding him so he can go home, if that earns me the right to get back to my wife, well then, then that's my mission.

2. I pray that our Heavenly Father may assuage the anguish of your bereavement, and leave you only the cherished memory of the loved and lost, and the solemn pride that must be yours to have laid so costly a sacrifice upon the altar of freedom.

Part IV Movie Review and Projects

Saving Private Ryan

Stephen Hunter

Searing, heartbreaking, so intense it turns your body into a single tube of **clenched** muscle, this is simply the greatest war movie ever made, and one of the great American movies. In one stroke, it makes everything that came before—with the exception of two or three obscure European variants on the same theme—seem dated and unwatchable. And it redefines the way we look at war.

Spielberg's ability to capture the **palpable** madness of all this borders on the incredible. The first 25 minutes of the film are creation of Omaha Beach from the point of view of an all-too-human Ranger captain, who's been here and done this, but not at this level of violence—is surely one of the great tours deforce of world cinema. From the **spillage** of viscera, the shearing of limbs, the gushing of blood and the psychotic whimsy of the bullets, to a final kind of fog of panic and soul-deep fear, he makes you glad it was your daddy's job, and not yours.

But Spielberg also understands war's deepest reality, which is that being there is not enough, and being willing to die for your country is also not enough; you have to be willing to kill for your country. So much of the battle **carnage** pictured in *Saving Private Ryan* is based on the craft of close-quarter, small-unit combat: It's watching men maneuver across terrain for geometrical superiority, hunting for a position to vector fire in on the enemy. He who shoots from the best position and brings the most fire to bear, he's the winner. The thermodynamics of infantry combat: Shoot well, shoot fast, shoot often.

As pure story, the movie has a swiftness to it that goes far beyond the sheer **fidelity** of the battle sequences. The narrative has been expertly configured; it moves us through a variety of experiences squad assault, town battle, sniper duel, a final stand against armored units-while at the same time keeping precise track of the overall story situation. Simultaneously, the personalities of the men are expressing themselves, in small ways. Even Damon's Ryan, who could be the font of sentimentality, turns out to be just another kid, low-key and quietly, furiously decent. (Damon, like all the actors, is excellent in this lesser role.) But it's no flashback-o-rama, in the fashion of "The Naked and the Dead", where each man's life is summed up in a banal recollection. Rather this is a point Spielberg makes over and over—these men have essentially given up on their **civilian** personalities—with the exception of the unit intellectual, the interpreter played by Davies—for the duration. They know the drill. They know what to do. They can hold it together. They've become, in Stephen Ambrose's wonderful term, complete Citizen Soldiers.

In this way, the film approaches its true subject, which isn't heroism, but duty, which is to say, repression. It's about men who make a conscious decision that the self does not matter; the "personality" is irrelevant; feelings are dangerous. Thus they become what they must be, to survive, to kill and to win: sealed-off beings locked away, hoarding their emotions, giving vent only to rage. They let nothing hang out because hanging out can get you killed. And Spielberg dramatizes this point twice, explicitly, in episodes where two soldiers yield to compassion. In this cruelest of world, the result is catastrophe. This movie is about a generation that put its heart on the shelf, dialed its minds down into a small, cold tunnel, and fought with its brains.

All the way through you can feel Spielberg flirting with **cliche**, almost daring us to recognize it and then at the last moment pulling it away from us and leaving us open-mouthed. But the biggest cliche that the movie assaults is the very conceit upon which war movies have been eternally built: It is the idea that somehow, combat is cool. There's always been an athletic grace to battle as the movies have portrayed it, a kind of **photogenic** sportiness. Even in the most violent of battle sequences, a little boy in you thought, "Hey, that's kinda neat." You know, dropping grenades on the German high command trapped underground in "The Dirty Dozen" or spray-painting Nazis red with your Thompson in "The Longest Day". And there was that Hollywood thing where the hero ran through blizzards of fire and somehow was never touched, because, after all, he was the hero.

That's all gone here. Not merely because of its gore but far more because of its cruelty, the war here will inspire no enlistees and no one will relive it in private later. It's flat-out terrifying, and the emotion it finally produces in you is more than any other film has gotten, but about one-thousandth of what the infantrymen of 1944 must have felt after one day on the line: utter exhaustion. You feel bled out, and at least emotionally, you have been.

So in the end, this one is for the boys of Pointe-du-Hoc, and also the boys of Utah and Omaha, Salerno, Monte Cassino, Iwo, the boys who took the long walk ashore at Tarawa through the Japanese fire, the boys whose last moments were spent in a flaming Fortress over Schweinfurt, or whatever, wherever, between the years 1941 and 1945. Take a bow, little guy, it says to them.

And to us, their inheritors, it says: Hey, look what your daddies did, what they went through, what they survived or didn't survive— and be proud. And it also asks us the hardest of all questions: Are we worthy of them?[1]

---

[1] Stephen Hunter. Saving Private Ryan [EB/OL]. (1998 – 07 – 24) [2018 – 02 – 03]. http://www. washingtonpost. com/wp – srv/style/longterm/movies.

New Words and Phrases：

clenched	adj.	紧握的
palpable	adj.	易于察觉的；可意识到的；明显的
spillage	n.	溢出
carnage	n.	大屠杀
fidelity	v.	忠诚；忠实；忠贞
civilian	n.	平民；老百姓；庶民
cliche	n.	陈词滥调；老生常谈
photogenic	adj.	上镜头的；易上镜头的；上照的

Project 1：Debate：Is War Necessary？

No doubt war is evil, the greatest catastrophe that befalls human beings. It brings death, destruction, disease, starvation, and poverty. One has only to look back to the havoc that was wrought in various countries not many years ago, in order to estimate the destructive effects of war. However, some people say war is necessary. A glance at the past history will tell now war has been a recurrent phenomenon in the history of nations. No period in world history has been free from the effects of war. Which side do you support? You may turn to the ideas in the following table.

War is necessary.	War is unnecessary.
War is a quick method to settle down conflicts.	Millions of people have been injured and even died in war.
War ensures human progress.	War brings devastating effect on humans' psychology.

Continued

War is necessary.	War is unnecessary.
War fuels the development of science and technology.	War leads to poverty and starvation.

Project 2: Interview at least 5 classmates and note down their viewpoints about whether there will be a World War Ⅲ.

1st interviewee: Major: Age: Gender:

Viewpoints: _____

_____

2nd interviewee: Major: Age: Gender:

Viewpoints: _____

_____

3rd interviewee: Major: Age: Gender:

Viewpoints: _____

_____

4th interviewee: Major: Age: Gender:

Viewpoints: _____

_____

5th interviewee: Major: Age: Gender:

Viewpoints: _____

_____

Chapter Ⅲ　Values and Assumptions

Introduction to the Chapter

To understand Americans' political, economic, social and even personal behavior, we must first know the dominant values in the USA. Bill Perry, in his book *A Look inside America*, places individualism as number one in his list of America's cultural values. Chapter Ⅲ will have an exploration of individualism.

Part Ⅰ　Cultural Foods

The Formation of American Individualism

The United States is regarded as the cradle of individualism. Actually individualism is not native in America. Tocqueville, a French socialist first used this term in his book *Democracy in America*. He gave a description rather than a definition of this new term: "Individualism is a mature and calm feeling, which disposes each member of the community to sever himself from the mass of his fellows and to draw apart with his family and friends, so that after he has thus formed a little circle of his own, he willingly leaves society at large to itself. "

The process of the industrialization, urbanization and modernization contribute to the formation of individualism. The Industrial Revolution accelerated the procedure for mass production. The manufacturing process is decomposed into several tiny sections without much manual labor as before. This great transformation finally made the industrial worker severely alienated.

Urbanization, a process in which the proportion of popularity in cities has been constantly increasing, is the second trend providing fertile soils to individualism. As an immigrant country, the United States' procedure of urbanization appeared to be more complex but manifest. People from Europe, Asia and Africa, have been voluntarily poured into the Big Melting Pot. The final product was "a multitude of separate corporations". During the progression, social differentiation then arose and people were not so liable to be connected together by loyal trusts, or somewhat of this kind as before. Contracts rather than handshakes have become so general to keep the relationship between people.

Another factor helping to accelerate the development of individualism is modernization, which is characterized as hundreds, even thousands of technologies and inventions having been put into service. So we draw the conclusion that the Industrial Revolution liberated people from their farmland, enabled them to seek their fortune in cities, and provided them with a great deal of newly invented articles which met their self-needs varying from one person to another.

The Embodiment of American Individualism

Self-reliance and pursuit of freedom should be the most important elements of American individualism. From the earliest age in America, children are encouraged to develop their sense of individual identity, achievement, and responsibility. Many Americans give their new born babies their own room and cot from the first day they come home from hospital. As the baby grows, every individual achievement is celebrated and encouraged at the youngest possible age, such as feeding himself, dressing himself, walking to a neighbour's house, talking on the phone politely, etc. Each individual is self-relied, responsible to himself/herself, thus entitled to the personal freedom. As a result, one of the worst insults in America is to suggest that someone relies upon others.

Equality: As stated in their *Declaration of Independence*, that "all men are created equal". Americans have a deep faith that in some fundamental way all people (at least all American people) are of equal value, that no one is born superior to anyone else. "One person, one vote", they say, conveying the idea that any person's opinion is as valid and worthy of attention as any other person's opinion. Quite different from Europe, the idea of equality in the United States assumes that everyone has equal opportunities rather than social positions. That is to say, each person has equal chance to achieve his success. No matter what a person's initial station in life, he or she has the opportunity to achieve high standing, and everyone, no matter how unfortunate, deserves some basic level of respectful treatment. Based on personal equality, individual competition then has evolved into a life attitude throughout the daily life of American people. In the United States, a fair social competition is protected by both political principles and organizational structures, ensuring an advantageous environment for personal equal competition.

Privacy: Also closely associated with the value they place on individualism is the importance Americans assign to privacy. Americans assume that people "need some time to themselves" or "some time alone" to think about things or recover their spent psychological energy. Americans have great difficulty understanding people who always want to be with another person, who dislike being alone. Americans tend to regard such people as weak or dependent... Americans' attitudes about privacy can be difficult for foreigners to understand. Americans' houses, yards, and even their offices can seem open and inviting, yet, in the Americans' minds, there are boundaries that other people are simply not supposed to cross. When the boundaries are crossed, the Americans' bodies will visibly stiffen and their manner will become cool and aloof.

Overall, individualism is a core value of American culture. Both for the American society and Americans, the noblest aspirations are closely linked with individualism. Americans believe in the dignity of the individual, respect individuals' independent thinking, independent judgments, as well as rely on its own strength to achieve personal interests. However, the extreme individualism has caused serious harm to the people and society. It's a long-term and difficult task for all the Americans to build an open, cooperative and creative new American individualism.

Part Ⅱ *The Shawshank Redemption*

The Shawshank Redemption is a 1994 American drama film written and directed by Frank Darabont, based on the 1982 Stephen King novella *Rita Hayworth and Shawshank Redemption*.

It tells the story of a banker Andy Dufresne, who is sentenced to life in Shawshank State **Penitentiary** for the murder of his wife and her lover, despite his claims of innocence. Over the following two decades, he befriends a fellow prisoner, **contraband smuggler** Ellis "Red" Redding, and becomes instrumental in a money **laundering** operation led by the prison **warden** Samuel Norton.

Over the years, he retains hope and finds ways to live out life with relative ease as one can in a prison. Eventually he gains the respect of his fellow **inmates**, and becomes influential within the prison. He conveys a message to all his inmates that while the body may be locked away in a cell, the spirit can never be truly imprisoned. In the end of the movie, Andy achieves his ends on his own terms.

New Words and Phrases:

penitentiary	n.	监狱;教养所
contraband	adj.	禁运的;非法买卖的

smuggler	n.	走私者;走私犯
launder	v.	清洗;洗黑钱
warden	n.	看守人;典狱官
inmate	n.	同院病人;同狱犯人

Part Ⅲ   Listening and Speaking Activities

Task 1: Watch and listen to the Clip: *1st Redemption*: *Win Beer for Inmates*. Write down the following sentences.

1. _____.

2. _____.

3. _____.

4. _____.

5. _____.

6. _____.

New Words and Phrases:

tar	v.	涂焦油
curry	v.	给……加咖喱粉;梳刷

Notes:

The Internal Revenue Service (**IRS**) is the revenue service of the United States federal government. It is a bureau of the Department of the Treasury, and is under the immediate direction of the Commissioner of Internal Revenue, who is appointed to a five-year term by the President of the United States. The IRS is responsible for collecting taxes and administering the Internal Revenue Code, the main body of federal statutory tax law of the United States.

Task 2: Work in groups, discuss how Andy put the seeds of "hope and freedom" into his cellmates through the following redemptions.

Win beer	
Play music	
Build a library	
Teach Tom	
Send a harmonica to Red	
Leave a secret letter for Red	

Task 3: Watch and listen to the Clip: *2nd Redemption: Play Music for Inmates*. Fill in the following blanks.

1. I have no idea to this day ＿＿＿＿＿＿＿＿＿.

2. Truth is ＿＿＿＿＿＿＿＿＿.

3. ＿＿＿＿＿＿＿＿＿.

4. I like to think they were singing about something so beautiful ＿＿＿＿＿＿＿, and ＿＿＿＿＿＿＿＿＿.

5. I tell you, those voices soared.

6. ＿＿＿＿＿＿＿＿＿ than anybody in a gray place dares to dream.

7. It was like some beautiful bird flapped into our drab little cage and ＿＿＿＿＿＿＿＿＿ and for the briefest of moments—

＿＿＿＿＿＿＿＿＿.

New Words and Phrases：

flap   v.   拍打

drab   adj.   单调的

Notes：

Institutionalization is an often-deliberate process whereby a person entering the institution is reprogrammed to accept and conform to strict controls that enables the institution to manage a large number of people with a minimum of necessary staff. Institutionalization is usually realized through depersonalizing from the beginning, destroying the self, forcing obedience, forcing a break with the outer world, physically assaulting them and controlling every aspect of their lives.

Task 4：Find examples in the movie to show how Shawshank institutionalize the prisoners. Interview four of your classmates on "my understanding on institutionalization". The following tips are for your references when preparing interview questions.

---

1. Do research in advance and have big picture of the topic in your mind.

2. Write a few experience-based questions to elicit the talk.

3. Ask 1~2 questions you know the answer.

4. Ask 1~2 questions you don't know the answer.

5. Prepare open-ended and conversational questions.

Example 1 :_____.

Example 2 :_____.

Example 3 :_____.

Task 5: Reflect on memorable sentences. Which sentences are still in your mind? Which sentence impresses you most? Why? Share your understanding of the sentences with your friends. Some sentences are listed below for your reference.

1. Hope is a good thing, maybe the best of things. And no good thing ever dies.

2. Some birds don't mean to be caged. Their feathers are just too bright.

3. Fear can hold you prisoner; hope can set you free.

4. It takes a strong man to save himself, and a great man to save another.

Part Ⅳ   Movie Review and Projects

Redeem Yourself

It is a strange comment to make about a film set inside a prison, but "The Shawshank Redemption" creates a warm hold on our feelings because it makes us a member of a family. Many movies offer us **vicarious** experiences and quick, superficial emotions. "Shawshank" slows down. It uses the narrator's calm, observant voice to include us in the story of men who have formed a community behind bars. It is deeper than most films; about continuity in a lifetime, based on friendship and hope.

Frank Darabont wrote and directed the film, basing it on a story by Stephen King. His film grants itself a leisure that most films are afraid to risk. The movie is as deliberate, considered and thoughtful as Freeman's narration. There's a feeling in Hollywood that audiences have short attention spans and must be **assaulted** with fresh **novelties**. I think such movies are slower to sit through than a film like "Shawshank", which absorbs us and takes away the awareness that we are watching a film.

Deliberate, too, is the dialogue. Tim Robbins makes Andy a man of few words, quietly spoken. He doesn't get real worked up.

He is his own man, capable of keeping his head down for years and then **indulging** in a grand gesture, as when he plays an aria from Mozart's "The Marriage of Figaro". (The overhead shot of the prisoners in the yard, **spellbound** by the music, is one of the film's epiphanies.) Because he does not volunteer himself, reach out to us or overplay his feelings, he becomes more fascinating: it is often better to wonder what a character is thinking than to know.

Roger Deakins' cinematography is tactful, not showy. Two opening shots, one from a helicopter, one of prison walls looming overhead, establish the prison. Shots follow the dialogue instead of anticipating it. Thomas Newman's music enhances rather than informs, and there is a subtle touch in the way deep bass **rumblings** during the early murder are **reprised** when a young prisoner recalls another man's description of the crime.

Darabont constructs the film to observe the story, not to **punch** it up or upstage it. Upstaging, in fact, is unknown in this film; the actors are content to stay within their roles, the story moves in an orderly way, and the film itself reflects the slow passage of the decades. "When they put you in that cell," Red says, "when those bars slam home, that's when you know it's for real. Old life blown away in the blink of an eye. Nothing left but all the time in the world to think about it. " Watching the film again, I admired it even more than the first time I saw it. Affection for good films often grows with familiarity, as it does with music. Some have said life is a prison, we are Red, and Andy is our redeemer. All good art is about something deeper than it admits. ❶

New Words and Phrases：

vicarious	adj.	代理的;发同感的
assault	v.	攻击,袭击
novelty	n.	新奇;新奇的事物
indulge	v.	满足于;沉溺于
spellbound	adj.	被咒语所镇住的;出神的;被迷住的
rumbling	n.	隆隆声;辘辘声
reprise	v.	重奏
punch	v.	开洞;以拳重击

Project 1： Do a survey among your classmates on their favorite movie and reasons for their recommendation.

	Favorite Movie	**Reasons**
Student 1		
Student 2		
Student 3		
Student 4		

Project 2： Compare your generation and your parents' generation in the following aspects to tell which generation is more individualized. You are supposed to give examples to back you up and elaborate the

---

❶ Roger Ebert. The Shawshank Redemption〔EB/OL〕. (1994 – 9 – 23)〔2016 – 11 – 5〕. https://www. rogerebert. com/reviews.

reasons behind.

	Parents' generation	Your generation
Self-reliance	1. 2. 3.	1. 2. 3.
Pursuit of freedom	1. 2. 3.	1. 2. 3.
Privacy	1. 2. 3.	1. 2. 3.
Equality	1. 2. 3.	1. 2. 3.

Chapter IV Education

Introduction to the Chapter

Education is the engine that drives the American dream of success. The opportunity to gain knowledge and skills that pay off in upward mobility has given hope to millions of Americans. Although the goals of education have undergone some shift with the changing concerns of the larger society, American faith in the school has persisted. A great majority of American population ticked "very important" when asked in the 1980s and the mid-1990s whether "America's strength in the future depends on developing the best education system in the world". This chapter will introduce American education at different stages.

Part I   Cultural Foods

Education in the United States is provided by public and private schools. Formal education in the U. S. is divided into a number of distinct educational stages. USA has a rather decentralized system of education. There is no national school system nor are there national framework laws that prescribe curricula or control most other aspects of education. The states, and, to a less extent, local school districts are responsible for the education of the children in their jurisdiction.

Primary education in the United States refers to the first eight years of formal education in most jurisdictions, often in elementary school. Preschool programs, which are less formal and usually not mandated by law, are generally not considered part of primary education. The first year of primary education is commonly referred to as kindergarten and begins at or around age 5. Subsequent years are usually being referred to as first grade, second grade, and so forth. Students graduating from the fifth grade, typically the last elementary year, are normally age 11.

Secondary education is often divided into two phases, middle or junior high school and high school. Students are usually given more independence, moving to different classrooms for different subjects, and being allowed to choose some of their courses (electives).

"Middle school" usually includes sixth, seventh and eighth

grade (and occasionally fifth grade as well). "Junior high" may include any range from sixth through ninth grades. The range defined by either is often based on demographic factors, such as an increase or decrease in the relative numbers of younger or older students, with the aim of maintaining stable school populations.

High school (occasionally senior high school) usually runs from 9th or 10th through 12th grades. Students in these grades are commonly referred to as freshmen (Grade 9), sophomores (Grade 10), juniors (Grade 11) and seniors (Grade 12). Generally, at the high school level, students take a broad variety of classes without special emphasis in any particular subject. Students are required to take a certain mandatory subjects, but may choose additional subjects to fill out their required hours of learning. High school grades normally are included in a student's official transcript for college admission.

Higher Education

Students completing high school may choose to attend a college or university, which offers undergraduate degrees such as associate degrees or bachelor's degrees.

Community college or junior college typically offers two-year associate degrees, although some community colleges offer a limited number of bachelor's degrees. Some community college students choose to transfer to a four-year institution to pursue a bachelor's degree. Community colleges are generally publicly funded (usually by local cities or counties) and offer career certifications and part-time programs.

Four-year institutions may be public or private colleges or universities. Some counties and cities have established and funded four-year institutions; examples include the City University of New York, City Colleges of Chicago, and San Francisco City College. Private institutions are privately funded and there is a wide variety in size, focus, and operation. Some private institutions are large research universities, while others are small liberal arts colleges that concentrate on undergraduate education. Some private universities are

nonsectarian and secular, while others are religiously-affiliated. While most private institutions are non-profit, a growing number in the past decade have been established for profit education.

Scholastic Assessment Test is widely used for college admissions in the United States. Introduced in 1926, its name and scoring have changed several times; originally called the Scholastic Aptitude Test, and now simply called the SAT.

The SAT is owned, developed, and published by the College Board and was intended to assess students' readiness for college. The SAT has four sections: Reading, Writing and Language, Math (no calculator), and Math (calculator allowed) to measure literacy, numeracy and writing skills that are needed for academic success in college. The test taker may optionally write an essay which, in that case, is the fifth test section. The total time for the scored portion of the SAT is three hours (or three hours and fifty minutes if the optional essay section is taken).

The SAT is offered seven times a year in the United States. In other countries, the SAT is offered four times a year. The only place in China where the SAT is offered for Chinese students is in Hong Kong. Candidates wishing to take the test may register online at the College Board's website, by mail, or by telephone, at least three weeks before the test date.

American College Testing is a standardized test used for college admissions in the United States. It was first introduced in

Nov. , 1959 by professor Everett Franklin Lindquist in University of Iowa as a competitor to the SAT. It is currently administered by ACT, a nonprofit organization of the same name. The required portion of the ACT is divided into four multiple choice subject tests: English, mathematics, reading, and science reasoning. The ACT is offered seven times a year in the United States and five times a year outside USA.

The ACT is more widely used in the Midwestern, Rocky Mountain, and Southern United States, whereas the SAT is more popular on the East and West coasts. The majority of colleges does not indicate a preference for the SAT or ACT exams and accept both, being treated equally by most admission officers.

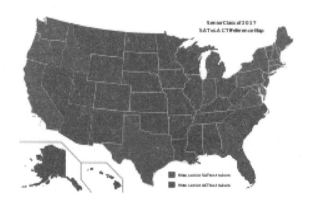

Part II   *The Dead Poets Society*

The Dead Poets Society is a 1989 American drama film directed by Peter Weir and starred by Robin Williams. Set at the conservative and **aristocratic** Welton Academy in Vermont in 1959, it tells the story of an English teacher who inspires his students through his teaching of poetry. The film was critically **acclaimed** and was **nominated** for many awards.

Neil Perry, Todd Anderson, Knox Overstreet, Charlie Dalton, Richard Cameron, Steven Meeks, and Gerard Pitts are senior students of the Welton Academy, an elite prep school, whose **ethos** is defined by the headmaster Gale Nolan as "tradition, honor, discipline and excellence".

The teaching methods of their new English teacher, John Keating, are **unorthodox** by Welton standards, including whistling the *1812 Overture* and taking them out of the classroom to focus on the idea of "carpe diem". He tells the students that they may call him "O Captain! My Captain!" in reference to a Walt Whitman poem, if they feel daring. In another class, Keating has Neil read the introduction to their poetry textbook, **prescribing** a mathematical **formula** to rate the quality of poetry which Keating finds **ridiculous**, and he instructs his pupils to rip the introduction out of their books, to the amazement of one of his colleagues. Later he has the students stand on his desk in order to look at the world in a different way. With Keating's help, the boys' self-consciousness is slowly awakened.

New Words and Phrases:

aristocratic	adj.	贵族的;贵族政治的;有贵族气派的
acclaim	v.	为……喝彩;向……欢呼
nominate	v.	推荐;提名
ethos	n.	民族精神;气质;社会思潮
unorthodox	adj.	非正统的;异端的;异教的
prescribe	v.	规定;开处方
formula	n.	公式;准则
ridiculous	adj.	可笑的;荒谬的

Part Ⅲ   Listening and Speaking Activities

Task 1: Listen to the following speech delivered by Mr. Nolan in the Clip: *Start of the New Semester.* Fill in the blanks with the missing words.

Headmaster: One hundred years ago, in ＿＿＿＿＿＿＿, 41 boys sat in this room and were asked the same question that now ＿＿＿＿＿＿＿ you at the start of each semester. Gentlemen, what are the four **pillars**?

Students: ＿＿＿＿＿＿＿＿.

Headmaster: In her first year, Welton Academy graduated five students. Last year, we graduated 51 and more than 75% of those went on to the Ivy League. This, this kind of accomplishment is the result of **fervent** ＿＿＿＿＿＿＿ taught here. This is why you parents have been sending us your sons. This is why we are the best ＿＿＿＿＿＿＿ in the United States.

New Words and Phrases:

pillar   n.   支柱

fervent   adj.   热烈的，强烈的

Notes:

The Ivy League is a collegiate athletic conference comprising sports teams from eight private universities in the Northeastern United

States. The conference name is also commonly used to refer to those eight schools as a group beyond the sports context. The eight members are Brown University, Columbia University, Cornell University, Dartmouth College, Harvard University, the University of Pennsylvania, Princeton University, and Yale University. The term Ivy League has connotations of academic excellence, selectivity in admissions, and social elitism.

Task 2: Watch the movie clip: *The Boys' First Classes by Different Teachers*, then answer the following questions.

1. Compare and tell the difference between the classes and teachers.

2. What's your first impression of Mr. Keating? Give some details to elaborate your points.

3. Why does Mr. Keating encourage "O Captain! My Captain!" and "carpe diem" in his first class?

New Words and Phrases:

dispel	v.	消除,驱散
fester	v.	溃烂, 化脓, 使……恶化
weakling	n.	虚弱的人
hymnal	n.	赞美诗集
stanza	n.	诗的一节
sentiment	n.	感情, 情绪
hormone	n.	激素, 荷尔蒙
invincible	adj.	无敌的,不能征服的

oyster	n.	牡蛎
iota	n.	极微小
fertilize	v.	施肥
daffodil	n.	水仙花

Notes：

1. **"O Captain! My Captain!"**：The poem is written by Walt Whitman in 1865. It was written to honor Abraham Lincoln, the 16th president of the United States. Walt Whitman was born in 1819 and died in 1892. He is among the most influential poets in the American canon, often called the father of free verse. His work was very controversial in its time, particularly his poetry collection *Leaves of Grass*, which was described as obscene for its overt sexuality.

O Captain! My Captain! our fearful trip is done;

The ship has weather'd every rack, the prize we sought is won;

The port is near, the bells I hear, the people all exulting,

While follow eyes the steady keel, the vessel grim and daring:

But O heart! heart! heart!

O the bleeding drops of red,

Where on the deck my Captain lies,

Fallen cold and dead.

O Captain! my Captain! rise up and hear the bells;

Rise up—for you the flag is flung—for you the bugle trills;

For you bouquets and ribbon'd wreaths—for you the shores a-crowding;

For you they call, the swaying mass, their eager faces turning;

O captain! dear father!

This arm beneath your head;

It is some dream that on the deck,

You've fallen cold and dead.

My Captain does not answer, his lips are pale and still;

My father does not feel my arm, he has no pulse nor will;

The ship is anchor'd safe and sound, its voyage closed and done;

From fearful trip, the victor ship, comes in with object won;

Exult, O shores, and ring, O bells!

But I, with mournful tread,

Walk the deck my captain lies,

Fallen cold and dead.

2. "**To the Virgins, to Make Much of Time**" is a poem written by Robert Herrick, an English poet in the 17th century. The poem is in the genre of *carpe diem*, Latin for **seize the day.** The opening stanza, one of his more famous, is as follows:

Gather ye rosebuds while ye may,

Old time is still a-flying;

And this same flower that smiles today,

Tomorrow will be dying.

Task 3: Watch the clip: *Rip the Pages.* Choose one of the following topics and discuss with your group members. You are advised to take different roles, such as the oral activity host, shorthand writer, the reporter and so on.

1. How do different students respond to Keating's suggestion?

Why?

_____

2. If you were a student in Keating's class, would you follow Keating's suggestion?

3. Mr. Keating says that poetry, beauty, romance and love are what we stay alive for. Do you agree or disagree? Why?

New Words and Phrases:

preface	n.	前言,序言
meter	n.	韵律
rhyme	n.	押韵
render	v.	给予,提供
horizontal	adj.	水平的
excrement	n.	粪便;废话
perforate	v.	穿孔
casualty	n.	伤亡;受害人
huddle	v.	拥挤,挤在一起

Task 4: Watch the movie clip: *Stand on Desks*, and fill in the blanks according to your comprehension.

Mr. Keating stands on the desk in order to remind students that _____. He explains that _____. He then encourages students to _____ instead of _____ when reading. Besides, he asks students to _____. At last, as an additional assignment, Mr. Keating requires students to _____ and _____.

New Words and Phrases:

strive	v.	努力,奋斗
resigned	adj.	顺从的
lemming	n.	旅鼠(北极的一种动物)

Notes:

Henry David Thoreau (July 12, 1817—May 6, 1862) was an American essayist, poet, philosopher, abolitionist, naturalist, tax resister, development critic, surveyor, and historian. A leading transcendentalist, Thoreau is best known for his book *Walden*, a reflection upon simple living in natural surroundings. His literary style interweaves close observation of nature, personal experience, pointed rhetoric, symbolic meanings, and historical lore, while displaying a poetic sensibility, philosophical austerity, and Yankee attention to practical detail. He was also deeply interested in the idea of survival in the face of hostile elements, historical change, and natural decay; at the same time he advocated abandoning waste and illusion in order to discover life's true essential needs.

Task 5: Watch the movie clip: *Walk in the Courtyard.* Work in groups of three and conduct an interview based on the situation given below.

A, a reporter from the Movie Review column of a newspaper, is interviewing two university students, B and C, for their ideas about the leading role Mr. Keating in the movie. The opinions elicited from the two students are opposed. The following words and expressions are for your reference in your interview.

insightful encouraging	put forward one's views	awaken one's inner self
mentor role model	open one's mind	explore the meaning of life
inspiring creativity	from a new perspective	challenge the authority
critical unconventional	illustrate the concept	advocate free thinking
passion ambition	arouse controversy	impose one's ideas on sb.

New Words and Phrases：

stroll	n.	散步，闲逛
stride	n.	大步走
ridicule	v.	嘲笑;愚弄
conformity	n.	一致；符合
herd	n.	兽群;庸俗的大众
diverge	v.	分歧;偏离

Task 6：Reflect on memorable sentences. Which sentences are still in your mind? Which sentence impresses you most? Why? Share your understanding of the sentences with your friends. Some sentences are listed below for your reference.

1. Just when you think you know something, you have to look at it in another way.

2. Even though it may seem silly or wrong, you must try!

3. Now, when you read, don't just consider what the author thinks, consider what you think.

4. If you noticed, everyone started off with their own stride, their own pace.

Part IV Movie Review and Projects

Shaking Up a Boys' School with Poetry

Vincent Canby

The time is 1959 and the place is the Welton Academy in Vermont. Welton is one of those expensive, tradition-bound boys' **preparatory** schools somewhat more beloved in, and more significant to English literature than American.

This being 1959, Welton has not yet been pressured into accepting young women or blacks. Its world is **insular**, that of the privileged white male who, if he is not already a **scion** of Old Money, will probably marry it. Into this rarefied atmosphere comes John Keating (Robin Williams), himself a Welton **alumnus**, who returns to teach English and to shake up the old school with his enthusiasm for poetry and his unconventional teaching methods.

One of the major problems with "Dead Poets Society", Peter Weir's dim and sad new movie, is that although John Keating is the most vivid and most complex character in it, he is not around long enough. He is really no more than the **catalyst** who brings about events over which he has no control.

"Dead Poets Society" which opens today at Cinema and other

theaters, is far less about Keating than about a handful of impressionable boys who become **bewitched** by Keating's **exuberant** assaults on the order of academe.

They include Neil Perry, a hard-working honor student who dreams of becoming an actor though his father insists that he go to Harvard to study medicine. Todd Anderson is so shy that he is frozen with fear when required to speak in front of the other students. Charlie Dalton has the makings of a true rebel and poet.

At Keating's first class of the new semester, he orders his students to tear out the preface in their poetry anthology. The offending pages suggest that the value of poetry can be measured in much the same way as the area of a **rectangle.**

Keating's credo is " Carpe diem!" (" Seize the day!"), because tomorrow we will all be food for worms. "We don't read and write poetry because it is cute, but because it is full of the passion of life. "

He mixes great **swatches** of Whitman with imitations of Marlon Brando and John Wayne. He recalls that when he was a boy, "I was the intellectual of 98-pound weaklings. I'd go to the beach and people would kick copies of Byron in my face. "

He drills his students mercilessly until each begins to perceive that, only by being out of step with others, will he have a chance to realize himself. With his encouragement, they revive a **clandestine** campus group of which Keating had been a founding member, the

Dead Poets Society. After hours, the members meet in a nearby cave, tell ghost stories, read Tennyson aloud and, in one case, play the saxophone.

In Mr. Williams's Keating, the movie has an authentic **approximation** of the kind of teacher who not only instructs, but also changes his students' lives. He is not, unfortunately, the center of Tom Schulman's screenplay, which moves with such deliberate predictability that one must walk very slowly not to walk ahead of it.

One would have to have been raised in a space station not to know that Keating must come into conflict with the other masters, and that one of his students will take his teachings to some fatal length. Even worse, Mr. Schulman and Mr. Weir seem to accept the Keating character at romantic face value. In allowing him to remain a sort of Mr. Chips, they leave unexplored the contradictory nature of his responsibilities. In fact, the Keating character is far more **culpable** than either he or the movie realizes.

In this fashion, the movie undercuts Mr. Williams's exceptionally fine performance, making the character seem more of a **dubious** fool than is probably intended.

Mr. Weir ("Picnic at Hanging Rock" "The Year of Living Dangerously" and "Witness" among others) obtains some very good performances from the younger actors, particularly from Mr. Leonard, and from Norman Lloyd who plays the headmaster.

Yet the director cannot resist **tarting** up the movie with the

fancified effects that pass for art: broad, eerie shots of birds taking off (or landing), night scenes prettily lighted from sources of illumination that must have been provided by the gods, along with scenes from an amateur production of "A Midsummer Night's Dream" in which Puck (for reasons that have more to do with the movie than the play) wears Christ's crown of thorns.

Like that crown, the movie is too heavy for its own good. ❶

New Words and Phrases:

preparatory	adj.	预备的;预科的
insular	adj.	孤立的;与世隔绝的
scion	n.	接穗;子孙
alumnus	n.	男校友;男毕业生
catalyst	n.	催化剂
bewitched	adj.	着魔的;被迷住的
exuberant	adj.	繁茂的;生气勃勃的
rectangle	n.	矩形;长方形
swatch	n.	样本,样品
clandestine	adj.	秘密的,私下的;偷偷摸摸的
approximation	n.	接近
culpable	adj.	有罪的;该责备的;不周到的;应受处罚的
dubious	adj.	可疑的;暧昧的
tart	v.	打扮

---

❶ Vincent Canby. The Dead Poet Society [EB/OL]. 1990 [2017 - 12 - 05]. http://movies. nytimes. com/movie/review.

fancify　　　v.　　　奇特地装饰

Project 1：Review the classes given by Mr. Keating in the movie. How do you think Mr. Keating inspires the students to break the conformity？

1st class：Hall lecture	
2nd class：Rip the pages	
3rd class：Stand on the desk	
4th class：Football and poem	
5th class：Barbaric yawp	
6th class：Stroll in courtyard	

Project 2：Conduct a social survey on the topic："Western high education in my eyes". You are supposed to interview six foreigners. Your survey should cover the following aspects. Write a 200-word survey report.

college enrollment　university classes　final exams　electives

after class activities　social service　volunteer　part-time jobs

teacher – student relationship　scholarship

graduation requirement

Interviewees	No. 1	No. 2	No. 3	No. 4	No. 5	No. 6
Nationality						
Gender						
Degree						

Chapter V　Family

Introduction to the Chapter

Family life is changing in the United States. With the increase of divorce, remarriage and cohabitation, the number of parents is declining. Because of the growth of single parent families and the decline in fertility rates, families are getting smaller and smaller. At the same time, the structure of the family has changed. With more and more mothers entering the labor force, more mothers become family members—in many cases, the main breadwinners of the family. As a result of these changes, the United States no longer has a dominant family form. Today, parents are raising their children in the context of an increasingly diverse and evolving family forms.

Part Ⅰ　Cultural Foods

Marriage in America

In the United States, the law of marriage is governed by individual states, and each state sets an "age of majority" at which individuals are not only free to decide when to enter into marriage by themselves, but also in what ages underage youths are able to marry with parental permission and/or judicial consent. In the long history of the United States, marriage laws have changed a lot such as abolishing the bans on same-sex marriage and interracial marriage. The median age for the first marriage has increased in recent years. The average age for men to get into a marriage contract was 23 in the early 1970s and 21 for women, and by 2009 it increased to 26 for women and 28 for men.

The reasons for getting married in the United States are the same as those in other countries, including love, a desire to have children, or economic security. Just as there are many reasons to establish a family, there are some causes for terminating it like annulment, divorce or death of a spouse. Divorce laws are different from states to states, and it irons out issues such as how the two spouses divide their property, how children will be looked after, and the obligations for the two spouses to support each other. In the past 50 years, divorce in the United States has become more and more prevalent. It was estimated that 20% of marriages would end in divorce within five years in 2005. The divorce rate in 2005 was four times that of 1955 and a quarter of children who are less than 16 years old are brought up by a stepparent. Marriages ending in divorce last for an average of 8 years for both men and women.

Roughly speaking, marriage is more legal than the other types of contracts between adults. A civil union refers to the formal combination between two persons of the same or of different genders, resulting in the same rights and obligations according to one view. The family partnership is a version of the civil union. Registration and recognition are the functions of states, regions, or employers, such unions may be available to heterosexual couples and sometimes even homosexual couples.

Family Structure

In the United States, the traditional family structure is thought as a family support system, in which two married persons provide care and stability for their own biological offspring. However, the two-parent nuclear family has become less common, and alternative forms of the family has become more prevalent. The family is established at birth, and builds up connections across generations. The extended family is composed of uncles, aunts, grandparents and cousins and plays economic and emotional roles for the nuclear family.

With the passage of time, the traditional structure has had to fit in with the very influential changes which include the single parent, divorce, teenage pregnancy, unmarried mothers, same-sex marriage, and the increase in the interest in adoption. Social movements such as stay-at-home father and the feminist movement have promoted the creation of alternative family forms, creating new versions of the American family.

Nuclear Family

The nuclear family has been regarded as the "traditional" family since the communism panic in the cold war in the 1950s. The nuclear family consists of a mother, father and the children. This kind of nuclear family has become less common and pre-American and European families have become more common form of a family.

Since the mid-1970s, the structure of the traditional nuclear family in the United States has begun to change. It was the woman in the family that has begun to make such a change. They decided to go out of their homes and start their own careers, not to live according to the male characters in their lives, including homosexual relationships, single parent families, adoptive individuals and extended family system of living together. The nuclear family also chooses to have fewer children than in the past.

Stepfamilies

The stepfamilies in the United States are becoming more and more familiar. The rate of divorce is rising and the remarriage rate is rising, too. As a result, two families make stepfamilies. Statistics show that 1,300 new stepfamilies are formed every day. More than half of American families remarry, that is, 75% of marriages end in divorce and remarry.

Extended Family

The extended family consists of grandparents, aunts, uncles and cousins. In some cases, the extended family is either living with the members of the nuclear family or replacing the members of the nuclear family. One example is that older parents move to live with their children because of their old age. This is a great request for the caregivers, especially the female relatives who choose to perform these responsibilities for their extended families.

Divorce

Likewise, divorce in the United States is regulated by state governments rather than by the federal government. All states acknowledge divorce by any other state. All states set a minimum time for divorce. All states allow for divorce on reasons such as irreconcilable differences, irremediable collapse and loss of emotion. Some states stipulate a period of separation before no-fault divorce. Mississippi, South Dakota and Tennessee are the only states that husband and wife need to agree with each other for the no-fault divorce. The rest of the states allow unilateral divorce without fault.

Since the mid-1990s of the last century, some states have covenant marriage laws that allow couples to divorce voluntarily, making it harder for them to divorce than they usually do. For example, couples who choose to conclude a contractual marriage may need to be consulted before they get divorced or submit their conflicts to mediation. In a state lacking such provisions, some couples signed contracts for the same obligations.

Cohabitation

In the United States, cohabitation refers to two or more intimate persons, who live together to share the common family life, but they are neither married nor civil unions.

In most parts of the United States, there is no legal cohabitation registration or definition. Therefore, demographers have developed various ways to identify cohabitation and measure the prevalence of cohabitation. The Census Bureau now describes the "unmarried couple" as "people over 15 years old, who have nothing to do with the householder, living together and having close personal relations with the householder". Before 1995, the Statistics Bureau identified any "irrelevant" heterosexual couples living together with other adults as "POSSLQ" or "Persons of Opposite Sex Sharing Living Quarters". The bureau is still reporting these figures to show historical trends. However, such measures should be loosened, because researchers reported that cohabitation often had no definite starting and ending dates, because people moved in or moved out of their homes, and sometimes at a specific moment, the definition of their residence arrangements was inconsistent. The population of cohabitation includes all age groups, but the average age of cohabitation is between 25 ~ 34 years.

In 2003, a study was conducted on the premarital cohabitation of women in monogamy. This study shows that, compared with women who don't want to have premarital sex or live together, the rate of divorce is not high among premarital sex workers and those who live only with the man they finally marry. For women in this category, premarital sex and cohabitation with the ultimate husband are only two steps to develop a firm and long-term relationship. However, these findings suggest that "only women with more than one close premarital relationship have a higher risk of marital breakage. For women with multiple premarital cohabitation, this has the greatest impact. "

A survey conducted by University of Denver in 2009 involving more than 1,000 married men and women in the United States found those who live together with their lovers before engaging in marriage had much lower quality marriages than other couples, and the possibility of breaking up was much greater. About 20% of the people who cohabited before their engagement suggested divorce.

Some people claim that people living together before marriage did not have satisfactory marriage and the opportunity for separation is higher. A possible explanation for this trend is that people who live together before marriage are doing this because they are worried about commitment, and when they have marital problems after marriage, this worry is more likely to turn into the final separation. Another explanation is that those who do not live together before marriage are often quite conservative in their religious views, and may have a more traditional view on gender roles, this attitude may prevent them from divorce for religious reasons or facing a marital crisis, although they have experienced problems as serious as those encountered by former cohabitants.

In addition, the behavior of living together can, in itself, lead to a more difficult attitude towards a happy marriage. For example, the results of a recent study suggest that "cohabitation partners may be less motivated to develop conflicts and support skills". An important exception is that cohabiting couples who have planned to marry in the near future have the same opportunity to stay together as couples who do not cohabit before marriage.

Part II *American Beauty*

American Beauty is a 1999 American theatrical film directed by Sam Mendes and written by Alan Ball. Kevin Spacey plays the role of Lester Burnham, a 42-year-old advertising director, who is in the middle age crisis, is fascinated by the best friend of his teenage daughter. Annette Bening plays the **materialistic** wife of Leicester. The movie is described by scholars as a satire on the concept of beauty and personal satisfaction in the middle class of the United States. The analysis focuses on the exploration of romance and paternity, sex, beauty, materialism, self-liberation and **salvation**.

New Words and Phrases:

materialistic	adj.	唯物的,物质的
salvation	n.	拯救

Part Ⅲ   Listening and Speaking Activities

Task 1: Watch and listen to the Clip: *Lester's Monologue*. Fill in the blanks.

I'd always heard your entire life _____ in front of your eyes the second before you die. First of all, that one second isn't a second at all. It _____ on forever likes an ocean of time. For me it was lying on my back at Boy Scout camp, watching _____ stars and yellow leaves from the maple trees that lined our street or my grandmother's hands and the way her skin seemed like paper. I guess I could be pretty pissed off about what happened to me, but it's hard to stay _____ when there's so much _____ in the world. Sometimes I feel like I'm seeing it all at once and it's too much. My heart fills up like a balloon that's about to _____. And then I remember to relax and stop trying to hold onto it. And then it _____ through me like rain and I can't feel anything but gratitude for every single moment of my little _____ life. You have no idea what I'm talking about, I'm sure, but don't _____, you will some day.

Task 2: Watch the Clip: *Lester and Carolyn's Quarrel.* Answer the following questions

1. Do you think Lester and Carolyn's marriage is a good match?

2. How does the conflict arise?

_____

3. Who should be blamed for their broken marriage?

_____

Task 3: Watch and listen to the Clip: *The Colonel's Family Dinner.* Answer the following questions.

1. Do you think it is a happy family with cozy atmosphere? If not, how do you draw the conclusion?

_____

2. What is Colonel's attitude towards the new neighbors?

_____

3. Do you think Colonel really agree with Ricky's opinion about homosexuality?

_____

4. Try to describe the character of the Colonel, and you can refer to the following vocabulary.

vain	overconfident	indifferent	elevated	emotional
selfish	pretentious	depressive	stern	earnest
boastful	low self-esteem	oppressive	solemn	conceited
unconcerned	cold and detached	grave	sincere	

Task 4: Watch the Clip: *Plastic Bags Dancing in the wind* and work in groups of five to:

1. Share notes with your partner.

2. Discuss the complex feeling contained in it.

3. Dub this scene.

Task 5: Watch the Clip: The Lester's Family Dinner and read the following conversation between Jane, Carolyn, and Lester, and note how the father tried to please the daughter, how the two expressed their feelings about each other and how the husband and wife accused each other of not being a good parent. Illustrate your findings with the sentences from the following script.

Jane: Mom, do we always have to listen to this elevator music?

Carolyn: No. No, we don't. As soon as you've prepared a nutritious yet savory meal that I'm about to eat, you can listen to whatever you like.

A long beat. Lester suddenly turns to Jane.

Lester: So Janie, how was school?

Jane: It was okay.

Lester: Just okay?

Jane: No, Dad. It was spec-tac-ular.

Lester: Well, you want to know how things went at my job. They've hired this efficiency expert, this really friendly guy named Brad, how perfect is that? And he's basically there to make it seem like they're justified in firing somebody, because they couldn't just come right out and say that, could they? No, no, that would be too... honest. And so they've asked us—you couldn't possibly care any less, could you?

Jane: Well, what do you expect? You can't all of a sudden be my best friend, just because you had a bad day. I mean, hello. You've barely even spoken to me for months.

Lester: Oh, what, you're mother-of-the-year? You treat her like an employee.

Carolyn: What?!

Lester: I'm going to get some ice cream. Honey, I'm sorry. I... I'm sorry I haven't been more available, I just... I'm... You know, you don't always have to wait for me to come to you...

Jane: Oh, great. So now it's my fault?

Lester: I didn't say that. It's nobody's fault. Janie, what happened? You and I used to be pals.

Task 6: Reflect on memorable sentences. Which sentences are still in your mind? Which sentence impresses you most? Why? Share your understanding of the sentences with your friends. Some sentences are listed below for your reference.

1. It's hard to stay mad when there's so much beauty in the world.

2. The minute you think of giving up, think of the reason why you held on so long.

3. I'm just an ordinary guy who has nothing left to lose.

4. You have no idea what I'm talking about, I'm sure, but don't worry, you will some day.

5. It's a great thing when you realize you still have the ability to surprise yourself.

6. There is nothing worse in life than being ordinary.

7. Today is the first day of the rest of your life? Well, that's true with every day except one: the day that you die.

Part IV   Movie Review and Projects

Movie Review

Nina Katungi

There are certain films that leave a mark in the industry that stand for new beginnings and *American Beauty* is one of them. *American Beauty* was Sam Mendes's first feature film. His previous experiences have been in the realms of English theatre, where he has been a huge success and has acclaimed an **impressive** amount awards. It is clear that his talents are not limited in just theatre but lucky for us in film too. *American Beauty* was a huge success and it won five Oscars in 2000 including "Best Picture" and "Best Direction", which is an outstanding achievement for Mendes as the film was his debut in feature film-making. The script was written by Alan Ball, a writer most well-known for his writing in television. His latest work can be seen in the successful series "True Blood". Alan Ball also won the Oscar, "Best Original Screenplay" for *American Beauty*.

Lester (Spacey) is married to Carolyn (Bening) and father of seventeen year-old Jane (Birch). Lester has been working for the same company for fourteen years, not the most **intriguing** of jobs but as a result of an endless comatose routine, he still shows up every day. The company's come to the point where it's decided to downsize and so Lester's job is at risk. Lester couldn't seem to care less and decides to **sabotage** any chance he has to stay. Lester's world is brought back to him when he meets his daughter's friend Angela. She becomes his only reason for continuing to endure his pitiful life, day in and day out.

While Lester eavesdrops outside his daughter's room he hears Angela saying to Jane that she finds her Dad attractive and that all he really needs to do is to work out a little. Lester decides to make some changes he heads to his garage where he searches for his weights that have clearly been buried away for a very long time. Lester also finds strength and hope in the new next-door neighbors' son Ricky.

Carolyn is Lester's estranged wife. Although they're still together, it's clear that their love deteriorated a long time ago. The most important thing to Carolyn however, is to portray an image of perfection despite the fact that behind doors their family has fallen apart. Carolyn is the master of all as she magically covers up the hate and unhappiness that she carries within herself. Carolyn is an estate agent, which is pretty much the only thing going in her life, although she has yet to be as successful as her rival Buddy whom she idolizes and eventually starts to have an affair with.

Jane is a typical teenager dealing with angst and insecurity that every person her age endures. Although it doesn't help that her parents are crazy and are too self-absorbed in their own lives to think about how she's doing. Angela is Jane's high-school friend who buries her insecurities by playing her good-looks against the not-so-good-looking and pretending to be sexually active, and wisely experienced beyond her age. Lester is the only one convinced by this beautiful goddess that she pretends to be. Jane's beauty is realized by her **infatuated** neighbor Ricky and she ends up receiving the true love and admiration to which Angela deeply longs for. Ricky opens Jane and Lester's world by showing them the beauty in absolutely everything. He becomes an inspiration especially to Lester. However in Ricky's home he is merely seen as a failure from his ignorant, **homophobic**, Marine Corps, father. His mother is a living ghost as result of her husband having sucked all life from her. Ricky finds solace and beauty in everything but his own home.

American Beauty is a perfect example where love, life, belief, and beauty all intertwine with one another. At the beginning of the film we find out that the main character, Lester is going to die. This film is obviously not the type of film structured with a build up to an unexpected ending. It becomes a "who done it?" mystery, which unravels through the events and interactions among the story's characters. The film is about change, fear, love, and life, a moment captured and realized in Lester's world, a moment where you know that if you died then and there it would be okay. This film has so many assets that help contribute to its absolute success. The cast involved are amazing, especially Kevin Spacey, Annette Bening, and Chris Cooper. Alan Ball had a wonderful, innovative story to tell and with Sam Mendes's fresh and bold vision this extraordinary was told. If you haven't seen *American Beauty* yet then you're missing out on one of the best U. S. films in the last decade. ❶

New Words and Phrases:

impressive	adj.	印象深刻的
intriguing	adj.	有趣的;迷人的
sabotage	v.	蓄意破坏
infatuated	adj.	热恋的;执迷的
homophobic	adj.	害怕同性恋的

Project 1: Work in groups and talk about your understanding of the following remarks about marriage.

1. Marriage makes or mars a man.

2. To marry means to half one's right and double one's duty.

3. An ill marriage is a spring of ill fortune.

4. Marriage is a lottery in which men stake their liberty and women their happiness.

5. He that marries for wealth sells his liberty.

6. Men are April when woo, December when they wed; maids are May when they are maids but the sky changes when they are wives.

---

❶ Nina Katungi. American Beauty 1000 Movie Review [EB/OL]. [2017 - 11 - 11]. http://www. wildsound - filmmaking - feedback - events. com.

Project 2: Write a movie review of *American Beauty*. Ask yourself the following questions and come up with a convincing thesis.

1. Does the film reflect current events or contemporary problems? This may be the way the directors engage in a bigger conversation. Find a way to link the content of the movie to the real world.

2. Does the film have a message, or does it try to draw a specific reaction or emotion from the audience? You can discuss whether it has achieved its own goals or not.

3. Is this film associated with you on a personal level? You can write a comment and weave some personal stories from your own feelings to make it an interesting story for your readers.

Chapter Ⅵ   Work Ethics

Introduction to the Chapter

Work ethic is a set of values based on hard work and diligence. It is also a belief in the moral benefit of work and its ability to enhance one's character. In the American get-it-done-yesterday society, your job and personal identity go hand in hand. Religious belief and new ideological trend and technology innovation all have great impact on Americans' work ethics. We will discuss the theme of work ethics in this chapter.

Part Ⅰ   Cultural Foods

Puritan Work Ethic

It seems Americans' desire for wealth is one that has lived in America as long as people have, which, actually, is not true. When the Puritans came to "the New World", they sought a "clean slate" to write their ethics and ideas upon. The Puritans, being a devout religious people, believed "that suffering is required to redeem our 'original sin' as human beings". This "no pain, no gain" mentality underlies American society even today.

The Puritans believed that honest toil, if persevered with, led to mundane and spiritual rewards. The modern equivalents of these archaic religious beliefs are: i) Hard work is the main factor in producing material wealth and; ii) Hard work is character building and morally good.

The "Puritan work ethic" is undeniably still alive today in America, and has spread around the world. Working hard means you can afford and collect more material wealth. Working hard means that you are a good person, you have a "good work ethic". Having a good work ethic automatically gives person credibility in American society. You are defined by what you own. Your car, your home, your clothing—all of these things define you. It is exactly "worthiness" that the Puritan work ethic is all about. The hard work ethic has conditioned Americans to see happiness as something that must be earned through toil. In effect, this is saying you have to suffer in order to get happiness, or to put it another way, you must be unhappy to be happy.

Why is the opposite of working hard being lazy? Once again, we can trace the answer back to the work ethics that were founded along with America. If working is salvation and worthy, then not working means abandonment and dishonor.

Competition in work is an instrument to prove one's ability in the workplace. Many Americans enjoy matching their energy and intelligence against those of others in a contest for success. People who like to compete are often honored by being called winners. On the other hand, those who do not like to compete and those who are not successful when they try are sometimes dishonored by being called losers.

The pressure to compete causes Americans to be energetic, but it also places a constant emotional strain on them. When they retire, they are at last free from the pressures of competition. But then a new problem arises. Some may feel useless and unwanted in a society that gives so much prestige to those who compete well. This may be one reason why older people in the United States sometimes do not have as much honor and respect as they have in other less competitive societies. In fact, generally speaking, any group of people who do not compete successfully, for whatever reason, do not fit into the mainstream of American life as well as those who do compete and succeed.

Media and Consumerism

American's highly commercialized and consumerism-oriented society has transformed the media into a breeding ground for corporate ideology as millions of messages saturate American people's lives each day. There is an extreme and obvious influence that consumerism in media has had in the USA; from logos to fast food chains, it has permeated the American lifestyle.

Americans are awash in media—television, movies, the internet, billboards, newspapers, magazines, radio, and newsletters. Individually and collectively American people spend more time with more media than ever before. This saturation is exactly how companies use the media to get consumers to spend. The breeding of want in American society drives the value of material objects way up. Americans work the whole lives to pay for their desire. Following this path from consumerism to why American people work so hard, they stumble upon the needs and shifts in technology.

Rising Problems

The decline of work ethic is now becoming a problem in USA. Researchers say America has lost sight of the virtues that comprise work ethic—the very things that helped build the young country.

The pursuit of happiness and the American Dream drove progress and innovation, but they came with unintended side effects. In many cases, for instance, healthy ambition has morphed into avarice. Urbanization and an emphasis on large-scale businesses means fewer and fewer kids are learning about work in the natural course of family life.

Technological advances that make life faster, more fun, more entertaining, and easier to navigate are also consuming American people's time and energy while eliminating avenues for learning vital concepts about work. And pop psychologists have pushed parents to focus on building self-esteem in their children, creating at least two generations of me-centric workers. No wonder so many employers are using terms like entitled, disengaged, unmotivated, and disloyal when describing their current workforce and potential labor pool.

Part Ⅱ *The Devil Wears Prada*

The Devil Wears Prada was released in 2006. It's an American comedy-drama film based on Lauren Weisberger's 2003 novel of the same name. Andrea is an aspiring journalist graduated fresh out of Northwestern University. Despite her **ridicule** for the shallowness of the fashion industry, she lands a job as junior personal assistant to Miranda Priestly, the editor-in-chief of *Runway* magazine. Andy plans to put up with Miranda's excessive demands and **humiliating** treatment for one year in the hopes of getting a job as a reporter or writer somewhere else.

Although the movie is set in the fashion world, most designers and other fashion notables avoided appearing as themselves for fear of displeasing U.S. *Vogue* editor Anna Wintour, who is widely believed to have been the inspiration for Priestly. Still, many allowed their clothes and **accessories** to be used in the film, making it one of the most expensively costumed films in history. Wintour later overcame her initial **skepticism**, saying she liked the film and Streep in particular.

New Words and Phrases：

ridicule	n.	嘲笑;笑柄;愚弄
humiliating	adj.	丢脸的;羞辱性的
accessory	n.	附件;饰品
skepticism	n.	怀疑论;怀疑的态度

Part III   Listening and Speaking Activities

Task 1: View and listen to the following clip: *Job Interview.*
Fill in the blanks with the missing sentences by Miranda. What's
your first impression of Miranda?

Emily: Human Resources sent her up about the new assistant
job, and I was preinterviewing her. But she's hopeless and totally
wrong for it.

Miranda: _____

_____.

Emily: Right. She wants to see you.

Andrea: Oh! She does?

Emily: Move! This is foul. Don't let her see it. Go! That's...

Miranda: _____.

Andrea: Uh, my name is Andy Sachs. I recently graduated
from Northwestern University.

Miranda: _____?

Andrea: Well, I think I could do a good job as your assistant.
And, um... Yeah, I came to New York to be a journalist and sent
letters out everywhere... and then finally got a call from Elias-
Clarke...and met with Sherry up at Human Resources. Basically, it's

this or Auto Universe.

Miranda: _____?

Andrea: Uh, no.

Miranda: _____?

Andrea: No.

Miranda: _____.

Andrea: Well, um, I think that depends on what you're...

Miranda: _____.

Andrea: Um, I was editor-in-chief of the Daily Northwestern. I also, um, won a national competition for college journalists... with my series on the janitors' union, which exposed the exploitation...

Miranda: _____.

Andrea: Yeah. You know, okay. You're right. I don't fit in here. I am not skinny or glamorous... and I don't know that much about fashion. But I'm smart. I learn fast and I will work very hard.

My first impression of Miranda: _____

_____

_____.

Task 2: View the Clip: *The Benefit Night.* Discuss with your group members and choose two most important tips on "how to improve peer relationship in work". Please explain why.

1. Choose your words carefully and listen actively when communicating.

2. Be responsible and make sure that you are doing your job well.

3. Remember that everyone is different and each person that you work with brings a different attribute to your workplace.

4. Show others that you are someone they can depend on.

5. Show your colleagues that you truly value their contribution to the workplace.

6. Try to display a positive attitude, even if you are feeling stressed or unhappy.

Two tips of greatest importance:

1. _____.

2. _____.

Task 3: View and listen to the following clip: *Celebration of James Holt*. Fill in the blanks with the missing words. Answer the question below.

Nigel: For 72 years, *Runway* has been more than a magazine. It has been _____ Miranda Priestly is the finest possible guardian of that beacon…setting a standard that inspires people across the globe. Ladies and gentlemen, I give you Miranda Priestly.

Miranda: Thank you, my dear friend. Bonjour. Thank you very much for _____ our dear friend, James Holt. But before I talk to you about James…and his many accomplishments…I would like first to share some news with you. Um, as many of you know... uh, recently Massimo Corteleoni... has agreed to _____ of the James Holt label... transforming the work of this visionary artist... into a global brand, which is really an exciting enterprise. *Runway* and James Holt share _____ ... chief among them, a commitment to excellence. And so, it should _____ that when the time came... for James to choose the new president of James Holt International... he chose from within the *Runway* family. And it's my great happiness today... to announce to you all that that person... is my friend and _____ ... Jacqueline Follet.

Jacqueline: Thank you. Merci.

Miranda: And now to the main event... our celebration of James Holt. We at *Runway* are very proud to have been...

Nigel: When the time is right, _____.

Andrea: You sure about that?

Nigel: No. But _____. I have to.

Why does Miranda make that decision?

_____

_____

Task 4: Work in pairs and make a dialogue based on the situation given below. While making up the dialogue, take both the advantages and disadvantages of the two alternatives into account.

> **Background situation:**
>
> Two college graduates, A and B, are exchanging views on career planning. A prefers to enter a company, start from the bottom and then work his/her way up. In contrast, B intends to set up his/her own business by getting a bank loan or financial aid from parents and relatives.

A: _____ .

B: _____ .

……

Task 5: Reflect on memorable sentences. Which sentences are still in your mind? Which sentence impresses you most? Why? Share your understanding of the sentences with your friends. Some sentences are listed below for your reference.

1. I am not skinny or glamorous and I don't know that much about fashion. But I am smart; learn fast and I will work very hard.

2. You are not trying. You are whining. You have no idea how many legends have walked these halls. And what's worse, you don't care. Because this place, where so many people would die to work, you only deign to work.

Part IV　Movie Review and Projects

Raise Yourself Up

Roger Ebert

When I was young there was a series of books about boys and girls dreaming of the careers they'd have as grown-ups. There were books about future coaches, nurses, doctors, pilots, senators, inventors, and so on. I also read the "*Childhood of Famous Americans*" series, but the "*Boy Announcer*" books were far superior, because they were about the childhood of me. I took a deep breath and began. This was the chance I had been waiting for!

The Devil Wears Prada is being positioned as a movie for grown-ups and others who know what, or who, or when, or where, Prada is. But while watching it I had the **uncanny** notion that, at last, one of those books from my childhood had been filmed. Call it Andy Sachs, Girl Editor. Anne Hathaway stars, as a fresh-faced Midwesterner who comes to New York seeking her first job. "I just graduated from Northwestern," she explains. "I was an editor of *The Daily Northwestern*!" Yes! It had been a thrill to edit the student newspaper, but now, as I walked down Madison Avenue, I realized I was headed for the big time!

Andy still dresses like an undergraduate, which offends Miranda Priestly (Meryl Streep), the powerful editor of *Runway*, the famous fashion magazine. Miranda, who is a cross between Anna Wintour, Graydon Carter and a **dominatrix**, stands **astride** the world of fashion in very expensive boots. She throws things (her coat, her purse) at her assistants, rattles off tasks to be done immediately, and demands the new *Harry Potter* in "three hours." No, not the new book in the stores. The unpublished **manuscript** of the next book. Her twins want to read it. So her assistant should get two copies.

Young Andy Sachs gets a job as the assistant to Miranda's assistant. That's Emily (Emily Blunt), who is terrified of Miranda. She is blunt to Andy, and tells her: She'll need to get rid of that wardrobe, devote 24 hours a day to the job, and hope to God she remembers all of Miranda's commands. I was impressed when I first saw the famous Miranda Priestly. She had the poise of Meryl Streep, the authority of Condoleezza Rice, and was better-dressed than anyone I'd ever met, except the Northwestern Dean of Women. And now she was calling my name! Gulp!

Young Andy has a live-in boyfriend, which wasn't allowed in those old books. He is Nate (Adrian Grenier), who has a permanent three-day beard and loves her but wonders what has happened to "the old Andy I used to know". I was heartbroken when I had to work late on Nate's birthday, but Miranda **swamped** me with last-minute demands. Emily, the first assistant, lives for the day when she will travel to Paris with Miranda for Spring Fashion Week. But then Emily gets a cold, or, as Miranda puts it, becomes "an incubus of viral plague". By this time Young Andy has impressed Miranda by getting the *Harry Potter* manuscript, and she's dressing better, too. Nigel took me into the storage rooms, where I found myself surrounded by the latest and most luxurious fashion samples! So Andy replaces Emily on the Paris trip.

"You are the one who has to tell Emily," Miranda kindly explains. Oh my god! I was dreaming! Paris, France! And as Miranda Priestley's assistant! But how would I break the news to Emily, who had dreamed of this day? And how could I tell Nate, whose own plans would have to be changed? Actually, by this time Young Andy has a lot of things to discuss with Nate, including her friendship with Christian (Simon Baker), a famous writer for New York magazine. Oh my god! Christian said he would read my clippings!

The Devil Wears Prada is based on the best-selling novel by Lauren Weisberger, which oddly enough captures the exact tone, language and sophistication of the books of my childhood: There was nowhere to wipe my sweaty palms except for the **suede** Gucci pants that hugged my thighs and hips so tightly they'd both begun to tingle within minutes of my securing the final button. This novel was on the New York Times best-seller list for six months, and has been published in 27 countries. I hope some of the translators left the word "both" out of that sentence. ❶

New Words and Phrases:

uncanny	adj.	神秘的;离奇的
dominatrix	n.	女性施虐狂;专横的女人
astride	adv.	跨着;两腿分开着
manuscript	n.	手稿;原稿
swamp	v.	使陷于沼泽;使沉没
suede	n.	小山羊皮

Project 1: View the whole movie and find examples to illustrate the work ethics displayed by Andrea. Write a 200-word report on the lessons you have learnt from the movie.

Work Ethics	Evidence Examples
Being punctual	
Being reliable	
Being responsible	
Being committed	
Being cooperative	
Being positive	
Being proactive	

Project 2: Interview at least 5 working people and tell how the following 7 habits of highly effective people can help us in our career development.

---

❶ Roger Ebert. The Devil Wears Prada [EB/OL]. (2006 – 06 – 29) [2016 – 12 – 12]. https://www. rogerebert. com/reviews/ the – devil – wears – prada – 2006.

1. Be proactive.

2. Begin with the end in mind.

3. Put first things first.

4. Think win-win.

5. Communication.

6. Synergize.

7. Innovation thought

1st interviewee: Profession: Age: Gender:

Viewpoints: _____

_____

2nd interviewee: Profession: Age: Gender:

Viewpoints: _____

_____

3rd interviewee: Profession: Age: Gender:

Viewpoints: _____

_____

4th interviewee: Profession: Age: Gender:

Viewpoints: _____

_____

5th interviewee: Profession: Age: Gender:

Viewpoints: _____

_____

Chapter VII   Welfare System

Introduction to the Chapter

Welfare system refers to the public assistance programs, providing cash or in-kind benefits for particular categories of the financially needy. Welfare system in the USA, developed mainly after WW Ⅱ and has undergone a long-time reform, now is very mature. It operates both on federal state level and is indispensible to people's everyday life.

Part I   Cultural Foods

Development of American Welfare System

American government learnt a hard lesson from the Great Depression from the 1930s to the 1940s. The government realized a nation-wide welfare system was necessary to protect people in the time of crisis. The depression originated in the U. S. , after the fall in stock prices in September 1929, and the stock market crash on October 29, 1929 . The Great Depression had devastating effects both on individual level and on the federal level.

In response to the Great Depression, President Franklin D. Roosevelt, who took office in 1933, enforced the New Deal. The New Deal was a series of domestic economic programs enacted in the United States between 1933 and 1936. It focused on what historians call the "3 Rs": Relief, Recovery, and Reform. That is Relief for the unemployed and poor; Recovery of the economy to normal levels; and Reform of the financial system to prevent a repeated depression.

The most important program of the New Deal was the *Social Security Act* in 1936. It established a permanent system of universal retirement pensions (Social Security, unemployment insurance, and welfare benefits for the handicapped and needy children in families without father present). Social Security Act established the framework for the U. S. welfare system. Roosevelt insisted that it should be funded by payroll taxes rather than from the general fund. He said, "We put those payroll contributions there so as to give the contributors a legal, moral, and political right to collect their pensions and unemployment benefits. With those taxes in there, no damn politician can ever scrap my social security program. "

In 1963, Lyndon Baines Johnson became the host of White House after Kennedy was assassinated. LBJ sponsored the largest reform agenda since Roosevelt's New Deal, which was called the "great society program". It encompassed movements of urban renewal, modern transportation, clean environment, anti-poverty, healthcare reform, crime control, and educational reform. The Great Society Program further developed the American welfare system.

Welfare Programs

Generally speaking, the welfare programs can be put into four categories. American current social welfare system is from the *Social Security Act* 1936, and after the introduction, gradually improves. The *Social Security Act* contains the following benefits: Retirement Benefits, Survivor's Benefits, Disability Benefits, Medicare Benefits, Unemployment Compensation, Public Assistance, and Maternal Children Benefits.

The second category is job insurance. Unemployment Insurance,

Worker's Compensation Program and State Disability Insurance go under this group. Public Service for Low Income Persons includes Food Stamp, School Lunch Program, Home Energy Assistance Program, and Public Low Income Housing. Medicaid is for the low income group. Seniors above 65 and those who are blind and severely crippled can benefit from In Home Support Service.

Part II *The Pursuit of Happyness*

The Pursuit of Happiness directed by Gabriele Muccino, is a 2006 American biographical drama film. It's based on a true story about a man named Christopher Gardner. While Gardner struggles very hard to make ends meet, his wife leaves him and he loses his apartment. Forced to live out in the streets with his son, Gardner continues to sell bone density scanners while concurrently taking on an unpaid internship as a stockbroker, with slim chances for advancement to a paid position.

The film features Will Smith as Gardner and was released on December 15, 2006, by Columbia Pictures. For his performance, Smith was nominated for an Academy Award and a Golden Globe for the Best Actor.

Part III   Listening and Speaking Activities

Task 1: View and listen to the Clip: *Job Interview*. Fill in the blanks with the missing words.

Chris: Chris Gardner. Chris Gardner. How are you? Good morning. Chris Gardner. Chris Gardner. Good to see you again. Chris Gardner. Pleasure. _____... trying to come up with a story... that would explain my being here dressed like this. And _____ that I'm sure you all admire here, like

_____, _____, _____, _____.
And I couldn't think of anything. So the truth is _____

Boss: Parking tickets?

Chris: And I ran all the way here from the Polk Station, the police station.

Boss: What were you doing before you were arrested?

Chris: _____.

Boss: Is it dry now?

Chris: I hope so.

Boss: Jay says _____.

Jay: He's been waiting outside the front of the building... with some 40-pound gizmo for over a month.

Boss: He said you're smart.

Chris: Well, I like to think so.

Boss: And you want to learn this business?

Chris: Yes, sir, I want to learn.

Boss: _____?

Chris: Absolutely.

Boss: Jay?

Jay: Yes, sir.

Boss: How many times have you seen Chris?

Jay: I don't know. _____, _____.

Boss: Was he ever dressed like this?

Jay: No. No. _____.

Boss: First in your class in school? High school?

Chris: Yes, sir.

Boss: How many in the class?

Chris: Twelve. It was a small town.

Boss: I'll say.

Chris: But _____, and _____. Can I say something? I'm the type of person...if you ask me a question, and I don't know the answer...I'm gonna tell you that I don't know. But I bet you what: _____, and _____. Is that fair enough?

Boss: Chris. What would you say if a guy walked in for an interview... without a shirt on... and I hired him? What would you say?

Chris: _____.

Task 2: Discuss with your teammates on "how does Chris win the interview?" and "what personality traits lead to his success in the interview?"

Task 3: Check **Yes** or **No** according to your understanding of the following tips for a job interview. Please explain why.

Tips	Yes/No
Do research on the company and the officers. Read the job description carefully.	
Arrive just in time for the interview.	
Put on fake smile while in the interview.	
Rehearse the interview with a friend.	
Write answers to the basic questions that you expect to be asked.	
Mention nothing of your weakness.	
Dress yourself as comfortable as possible.	
Introduce yourself as detailed as possible.	
Ask no questions in the interview.	
Remain respectful, professional, confident, and be calm.	

Task 4: View and listen to the Clip: *The First Day in the Company*. Fill in the blanks with the missing words.

The 1,200 building is Medley Industrial and Sanko Oil. The building _____ is Lee-Ray Shipping. In a couple of weeks, you'll get call sheets…with the phone numbers of employees…from every _____ in the financial district. You will be pooling from 60 Fortune companies. You will mainly be _____.

But if you have to have lunch with them, have breakfast with them…_____, do whatever it takes to familiarize them… with our packages. We need you to _____ …to one of our many financial plans. In essence, you reel them in… _____. Some of you are here because you know somebody. Some of you are here because you think you're somebody. There's one guy in here who's gonna be somebody. That person is gonna be the guy… who can turn this into this. Eight hundred thousand in _____. You, you, help me hand these out. This is going to be your bible. You'll eat with it. You'll drink with it. It was simple. X number of calls equals _____. X number of prospects equals X number of customers. X number of customers equals X number of dollars… in the company' pocket. Your _____. Last year, we had an intern score a 96.4 percent on the written exam. It's not a _____. It's an evaluation tool we use to separate applicants. Be safe, _____.

Task 5: Reflect on memorable sentences. Which sentences are still in your mind? Which sentence impresses you most? Why? Share your understanding of the sentences with your friends. Some sentences are listed below for your reference.

1. I'm the type of person, if you ask me a question, and I don't

know the answer, I'm gonna tell you that I don't know. But I bet you what: I know how to find the answer, and I'll find the answer.

2. Don't ever let someone tell you, you can't do something. Not even me. You got a dream, you got to protect it. People can't do something themselves, they want to tell you that you can't do it. You want something, go get it. Period.

3. We all have to deal with mountains. You know mountains that go way up high. And mountains that go deep and low. We know what those mountains are, here at Glide. We sing about them. Lord, don't move that mountain; give me strength to climb it. Please don't move that stumbling block. But lead me, Lord, around it, my burdens, they get so heavy seems hard to bear. But I won't give up. Because you promised me you'd meet me at the altar of prayer. Lord don't move that mountain, but give me strength to climb it.

4. Maybe happiness is something that we can only pursue. And maybe we can actually never have it, no matter what.

Part IV   Movie Review and Projects

A Good Dad's Way

"You're a good papa." Those tenderhearted words from Christopher to his father as they spend the night in a homeless shelter **poignantly** capture the essence of *The Pursuit of Happiness*. Chris isn't perfect, but one emotional scene after another clearly demonstrates his drive to protect and provide for his son.

Physical affection (hugs and kisses) and heartfelt moments mark their relationship. Chris repeatedly asks Christopher to trust him, and Dad proves that he's worthy of that trust. When Linda threatens to leave, Chris demands that their son stay with him. He knows he'll be a better parent than she would be—a reality to which Linda **grudgingly** acquiesces. Later, Christopher asks his dad, "Did Mom leave because of me?" Chris responds, "Mom left because of Mom. And you didn't have anything to do with that."

Actively concerned about his son's education and mental development, Chris gets upset when he learns that Christopher's day care provider, Mrs. Chew, lets the kids watch *Bonanza* and *Love Boat*. Chris teaches his son word meanings, such as the difference between "probably" and "possibly", and the fact that "happiness" is misspelled on his daycare's sign. (It's mistakenly spelled with a "y"; the film's title intentionally follows suit.)

Chris encourages his boy to make a birthday wish-list, and then gets him a basketball as a present. And one of the film's most powerful scenes comes when Christopher is trying to shoot **hoops** with his new ball. After a strong-but-**errant** shot, Dad critically informs him, " You'll excel at a lot of things, but not 'basketball'," perhaps projecting his own experience onto his son. Christopher immediately lives down to Dad's low expectations and takes a weak shot. Noticing his son's downcast countenance, Chris realizes his error and rectifies the situation, saying, "Don't ever let somebody tell you that you can't do something. Not even me. All right? You got a dream? You gonna protect it. People can't do something themselves, they want to tell you that you can't do it. You want something, go get it. Period. "

A harrowing night of homelessness finds the pair killing time at a deserted Bay Area Rapid Transit stop. Father and son imagine that Dad's bone-density machine is actually a time-travel device that takes them back to the time of the dinosaurs. Christopher gleefully joins in the make-believe game as they flee from a T-Rex into a "cave"—a public restroom where they spend the night. Dad holds the door shut with his foot, and tears stream down his face as he watches his innocent son sleep on his lap.

In addition to such a strong father-son relationship, *The Pursuit of Happiness* also presents the American Dream as an achievable reality. It begins when Chris asks a Dean Witter broker (who he sees getting out of a bright-red Ferrari) what's needed to do the job. The answer he gets back is this: "You've got to be good with numbers and good with people." Chris believes he has those skills and aggressively pursues executives at Dean Witter once he discovers internships are available.

He **hounds** his first contact, Jay Twistle, until the man pays attention to him. Several other people at Dean Witter give Chris chances to prove himself, though they aren't really duty-bound to do so. And even though he's virtually broke, Chris gives $5 to one of his rich superiors so he can pay for cab fare. Later, Chris misses an appointment with an executive (for reasons beyond his control), and goes to the man's house to apologize. The exec Walter Ribbon, in turn, kindly invites Chris and Christopher to share his skybox at a 49ers game.

Inspirational isn't a word I would normally choose to describe a great movie, as it **conjures** up connotations of something **sappy** or overly sentimental. Nevertheless, I think that's the word that best captures Will Smith's powerful portrayal of real-life father and pull-yourself-up-by-your-bootstraps worker Chris Gardner. ❶

---

❶ The Pursuit of Happiness [EB/OL]. [2017 – 04 – 22]. https://www. pluggedin. com/movie – reviews.

New Words and Phrases:

poignantly	adv.	深刻地;辛辣地;令人辛酸地
grudgingly	adv.	勉强地;不情愿地
hoop	n.	箍;铁环
errant	adj.	周游的;偏离正路的
hound	v.	追猎;烦扰;激励
conjure	v.	念咒召唤;想象
sappy	adj.	愚笨的

Project 1: Do a research on the American welfare programs and fill in the chart below.

Programs	Beneficiary Group	Contents
Retirement Benefits		
Unemployment Compensation		
Unemployment Insurance		
Food Stamp		
School Lunch Program		
Medicare Benefits		

Project 2: Read the lyrics of the theme song in the movie *The Pursuit of Happiness*. Write a report on your understanding of the song.

A Father's Way

I build a fence around you in a father's way

I try to feel what it is you'll be going through

Co's I've played many ways

When you grow, how much will it take to slow you down...

Half the way?

Do my best to feed you and I do what's right

I try to find the words that I'll say to you

When you come home tonight

And if so, how hard will we cry before our sound

Fades away?

One day when the fence is not so high

The road you took

How far will you go?

How high will you climb?

And when all in life's unfair

Are you strong enough to find another way, find another way

find another way?

A Father's way

I build a fence around you in a father's way

Just like the one who used to preach to me

Now I've become that way

But you know

How soft now the hand that used to strike

To the heart

One day when the fence is not so high

The road you took

How far will you go?

How high will you climb?

And when all in life's unfair

Are you strong enough to find another way, find another way

find another way?

There's no way

You will stay

There's no way

I know you,

There's no way.

You will stay

There's no way

I know you.

Chapter VIII   Mass Media

Introduction to the Chapter

The powerful mass media in the United States consist of newspapers, magazines, radio, television, and internet along with reporters and correspondents with their recording devices and cameras running after celebrities. Once, the world of mass media was dominated by newspapers and magazines, whose owners were moguls in their own right. But the gadgets of radio and television opened up a world of possibilities and accordingly the media was divided into print and electronic versions. The recent emergence of the Internet has even added much more strength to electronic media in no uncertain terms.

Part I   Cultural Foods

The Print Media

For almost a century, media was synonymous with print media since newspapers and magazines were the only sources of mass communication and for dissemination of information. The first U. S.

newspaper, published on September 25, 1690, lasted only one day before suppressed by British colonial authorities. Since then, the print media had undergone rapid development because of faster printing methods, lower prices, and the lure of advertising money: by the end of World

War II, approximately two-thirds of American adults read a daily newspaper on an average weekday. The top five daily newspapers by circulation in America are *the Wall Street Journal*, *USA Today*, *the New York Times*, *Los Angeles Times*, and *the Washington Post*.

The similar developments that promoted newspaper circulation also marked the beginning of mass appeal magazines. Since newspapers reached only local audiences, popular magazines could attract advertisers eager to reach a national audience for their products. By the early 1900s, magazines had become one of the dominant marketing devices. The most influential magazine, *Time*, was launched in 1923. Aiming at people too busy to keep up with a daily newspaper, *Time* was the first magazine to organize news into separate departments such as national affairs, business and science. Another magazine, *Newsweek*, using much the same format, was started in 1933. Other prominent news weeklies are *Business Week*, *U. S. News* and *World Report*.

Radio and TV

The launch of commercially licensed sound broadcasting in the

United States in 1920 ended the print monopoly over the media and opened the doors to the more immediate and prevalent electronic media. By 1928, the United States had three national radio networks— two owned by NBC (the National Broadcasting Company), and one by CBS (the Columbia Broadcasting System).

Though mostly for entertainment, radio's instant, on-the-spot reports of dramatic events attracted huge audiences, especially throughout the Great Depression of the 1930s and World War Ⅱ. President Franklin Roosevelt recognized the potential of radio to reach the American public. During his four terms (1933—1945), his radio "fireside chats", a series of 30 evening radio addresses, informed the nation on the progress of policies to counter the Depression and on developments during World War Ⅱ.

After World War Ⅱ, television's visual images took place of the audio-only limitation of radio as the predominant entertainment and news vehicle. Radio adapted to the new situation by replacing entertainment programs with a format of music interspersed with news and features. In the 1950s, automobile manufacturers started offering car radios as standard accessories, and thus radio received a big boost as Americans tuned in their car radios as they drove to and from work.

Television began invading American homes in World War II. The idea of seeing "live" shows in the living room was immediately attractive. Almost every American household (98% in 1999) has at least one TV set. Seven in ten Americans in 1991 reported getting most of their news from TV. Three large privately-owned networks— NBC, CBS and ABC—claimed 90 percent of the TV market from the 1950s through the 1970s with free broadcasts.

In this period, a term "couch potato" was coined to describe someone who leads a sedentary lifestyle with very little to no exercise and spends a great deal of time watching television. Couch potato was first used during a telephone conversation by Tom Iacino of Pasadena, California on July 15, 1976, when he humorously advocated vegging on the couch while eating junk food. Robert Armstrong, a friend of Iacino's and a comic artist, took the term and created a cartoon of a couch with a potato on it.

The Internet

Speed and timeliness were once the advantages of newspapers. The wire services built their reputations on being first with the big stories, which people typically found in their local papers. The immediacy of television took that edge from the printed press. Now the Internet has established its own advantages of speed and timeliness.

The Internet has strengthened the traditional watchdog functions of journalism by offering reporters efficient ways to pry and probe more deeply for information. The ability to search documents, compile background and historical context, and identify authoritative sources has expanded the reporter's toolbox. It also has introduced a fundamentally different culture built on interactivity, fewer rules, and fewer limits.

Therefore, the Internet poses a fundamental challenge to previous models of mass communication. Its bottom-up, decentralized, networked, and interactive characteristics stand in sharp contrast to the top-down, centralized, linear, and mostly mono-directional mass communication models of the past. As such, the Internet holds the promise of sustainable development, because it can contribute to coordinating global resources with local needs. For that potential to be realized, the Internet has to be considered as a public resource, and must not fall under the control of corporations or governments.

Part II   *The Truman Show*

The Truman Show is a 1998 American satirical science fiction film directed by Peter Weir, and written by Niccole. The film stars Jim Carrey as Truman Burbank, adopted and raised by a corporation inside a simulated television show revolving around his life, until he discovers it and decides to escape.

In this movie, Truman is a man whose life is a fake one. The place he lives is in fact a big studio with hidden cameras everywhere, and all his friends and people around him, are actors who play their roles in the most popular TV-series in the world: The Truman Show. Truman thinks that he is an ordinary man with an ordinary life and has no idea about how he is exploited. Until one day... he finds out everything. Will he react?

Part Ⅲ   Listening and Speaking Activities

Task 1: View and listen to the Clip: *Prologue by Christof*, complete the sentences with the aid of the cue words.

1. _____ become bored with _____ phony emotions.

2. _____ pyrotechnics and _____.

3. _____ counterfeit.

4. _____. No _____;
no _____.

5. _____ Shakespeare, but _____.

_____.

New Words and Phrases:

phony	adj.	假的,欺骗的
pyrotechnics	n.	烟火制造术
counterfeit	n.	赝品;冒牌货;伪造品

Task 2: View the Clip: *Truman's Try to Escape from Seahaven*. Take notes and do the story relay race in group of 3 to complete Truman's tries to escape from Seahaven.

Turman's Try	How was Truman stopped	the End
Fly to Fiji		
Go to Chicago by grey hound		
Drive to New Orleans		

Task 3: View and listen to the Clip: *The True Talk*. Fill in the blanks and answer the following questions.

Now in its 30th great year, it's The Truman Show! What a week! I was on _____ the entire time. I'm your host, Mike Michelson. Welcome to Tru-Talk, our forum for issues _____ the show. Tonight, something very special: An _____ interview with the show's creator. Let's _____ the 221st floor of the Omni-Cam Ecosphere. There we'll find the world's greatest tele-visionary. The designer of the world within a world that is Seahaven: Christof. I'd like to thank you for _____ this interview. We know your schedule is _____, and how you guard your privacy. This, sir, is indeed an honor.

1. Why was Truman's father manufactured to die?

_____

2. How did Christof explain the father's absence for 22 years?

_____

3. How did Truman become the first baby adopted by a corporation?

_____

4. In what way does the Truman Show TV program make itself profitable?

_____

5. Do you think Christof is a liar? Why or Why not?

_____

Task 4: View and listen to the Clip: *Goodbye to Seahaven*. Complete the dialogue between Truman and Christof. Role play the last scene in pairs.

Christof: Truman … You can speak. I can hear you.

Truman: Who are you?

Christof: I'm the creator of a TV show. _____.

Truman: Then who am I?

Christof: You're the star.

Truman: Was nothing real?

Christof: You were real. That's what made you so good to watch. Listen, Truman. There's no more truth out there than in the world I created for you. _____. But in my world, you have nothing to fear. I know you better than you do.

Truman: _____.

Christof: You're afraid. That's why you can't leave. It's okay, Truman. I understand. I have been watching you your whole life. I was watching _____. I was watching _____. I watched you _____. The episode when you lost your first tooth. You can't leave, Truman.

Truman: Please, God.

Christof: You belong here. You can do it. With me. Talk to me. Say something. Say something, damn it! You're on TV. You're live to the world!

Truman: _____.

Task 5: Reflect on memorable sentences. Which sentences are still in your mind? Which sentence impresses you most? Why? Share your understanding of the sentences with your friends. Some sentences are listed below for your reference.

1. I want to get away. See some of the world.

2. We accept the reality of the world with which we're presented.

3. Maybe I'm being set up for something. Like your whole life has been building towards something.

4. No way, mister. You're going to the top of this mountain, broken legs and all.

Part IV Movie Review and Projects

A Controlled World

Roger Ebert

The Truman Show is founded on an enormous secret that all of the studio's advertising has been determined to reveal. I didn't know the secret when I saw the film, and was able to enjoy the little doubts and wonderings that the filmmakers so carefully planted.

Those fortunate audience members will be able to appreciate the **meticulous** way director Peter Weir and writer Andrew Niccol have constructed a jigsaw plot around their central character, who doesn't suspect that he's living his entire life on live television. Yes, he lives in an **improbably** ideal world, but I fell for that: I assumed that the movie was taking a sitcom view of life, in which neighbors greet each other over white **picket** fences, and Ozzie and Harriet are real people.

Actually, it's Seaside, a planned community on the Gulf Coast near Tampa. Called Seahaven in the movie, it looks like a nice place to live. Certainly Truman Burbank doesn't know anything else. You accept the world you're given, the filmmakers suggest; more thoughtful viewers will get the buried message, which is that we accept almost everything in our lives without examining it very closely. Truman works as a sales executive at an insurance company, is happily married to Meryl, and doesn't find it suspicious that she describes household products in the language of TV commercials. He is happy, in a way, but uneasiness **gnaws** away at him. Something is missing, and he thinks perhaps he might find it in Fiji, where Lauren, the only woman he really loved, **allegedly** has moved with her family.

Truman's world is controlled by a TV producer named Christof, whose control room is high in the artificial dome that provides the sky and horizon of Seahaven. He discusses his programming on talk shows, and dismisses the protests of those who believe Truman is the victim of a cruel **deception**. Meanwhile, the whole world watches Truman's every move and some viewers even leave the TV on all night, as he sleeps.

I enjoyed *The Truman Show* on its levels of comedy and drama; I liked Truman in the same way I liked Forrest Gump—because he was a good man, honest, and easy to sympathize with.

But the underlying ideas made the movie more than just entertainment. It brings into focus the new values that technology is forcing on humanity.

Because we can engineer genetics, because we can telecast real lives—of course we must, right? But are these good things to do? The irony is, the people who will finally answer that question will be the very ones produced by the process. ❶

New Words and Phrases:

meticulous	adj.	小心翼翼的
improbably	adv.	不像真实地
picket	n.	尖木桩
gnaw	v.	咬;折磨;侵蚀
allegedly	adv.	据称
deception	n.	欺骗

Project 1: Review the movie and work in groups to complete the chart below.

What kind of life does Truman lead?	What are the commercials you see?	What are the signs that Seahaven is a fake world?

---

❶ Roger Elbert. A Controlled World [EB/OL]. (1998 – 06 – 05) [2017 – 11 – 15]. https://www.rogerebert.com/reviews.

Project 2: Conduct a social survey on the audience comments on the Chinese true man show TV programs. Write a 200-word survey report.

Programs	TV	Positive Comments	Negative Comments
Go Fighting			
Let's Go			
Running Man			
Twenty-Four Hours			
Singer			

Chapter IX   Popular Culture

Introduction to the Chapter

The culture of the United States of America mainly originated from Western culture (European), but it is influenced by the multicultural spirit of Polynesian, Asian, Native Americans, African, Latin American people and their cultures. It also has its own cultural and social features, such as social habits, art, dialects, music, cooking and folklore. The United States of America is a country with diverse races and ethnics. It is the result of large-scale migration of many countries in its history. Many American cultural elements, especially the popular culture, have spread to all parts of the world through modern mass media.

Part I   Cultural Foods

Music Culture

American music reflects the multiracial population of the country in a variety of styles. It is a mixture of music influenced by Scotland, West Africa, Ireland, and the continent of Europe. The country's most famous music genres are hip hop, jazz music, country music, rhythm and blues, ragtime, soul, barber shop, heavy metal, punk, disco, house, popular music, techo, experimental, rock and roll. The United States has the world's largest music market, with a total retail sales of $4,898.3 million dollars in 2014, and its music can be heard all over the world. Since the early twentieth century, some forms of American pop music have gained access to the audience around the world.

The Native Americans were the earliest inhabitants of the land called the United States today and played its first music. Since seventeenth century, immigrants from Spain, Britain, Ireland, France, and Germany have begun to pour in and bring new styles and musical instruments. The African slaves brought musical traditions, and every subsequent wave of immigrants contributed to a melting pot.

Many of the roots of modern pop music can be traced back to

the appearance of African American blues at the end of the nineteenth century and the development of the gospel music in the 1920s. The base of African American pop music uses elements derived from European and Aboriginal music. The original white settlers' musical traditions, such as country and blue grass, also have a strong African ancestry. The United States has also seen documented folk music and recorded popular music produced in the ethnic style of Scottish, Ukrainian, Irish, Hispanic, Polish, and Jewish communities.

Many American cities and towns have a vibrant musical scene, which in turn supports a lot of regional musical styles. In addition to Chicago, Philadelphia, Seattle, Portland, New Orleans, New York, San Francisco, Miami, Detroit, Minneapolis, Atlanta, Nashville, Austen and Los Angeles Music Center, New Jersey, many other smaller cities like Asbury Park also have their own unique style of music.

In the second half of American history, the relationship between American and European music has been a topic discussed by American musicians until modern times. Some people urge to adopt a more pure European technology and style, which sometimes are considered to be more elegant or graceful, while others strongly advocate a musical nationalism that celebrates the unique American style.

In the Civil War and in the aftermath of it, American literature, art, and music flourished. The amateur music combination of this age can be seen as the birth of American pop music. David Evan, a music writer, describes these early amateur bands as "classic depth and drama combined with unwanted skills, avoiding complexity and expressing directly. " If it is a vocal music, these words will be English, although those who claim that English is a snob of an unavailable language. To a certain extent, this is part of the awakening of the America after the Civil War. During this period, American painters, writers and serious composers discussed the theme of the United States. At this time, the roots of blues, gospel, jazz and country music began to take shape. In the twentieth century, these music became the core of American pop music and evolved into rhythms and styles such as rhythm and blues, rock and roll and hip-hop music.

Sports Culture

In the United States, sports are an important part of national culture and the four major professional sports alliances in the U. S. are MLB, NBA, NFL and NHL. The professional sports market in the United States is about $69 billion, about 50% larger than the total of Europe, the Middle East and Africa. All major sports teams operate as a franchise in the  league, which means that if the owners believe that there will be economic benefits, the team may move to a different city, but the franchise usually go through some form of league level approval. All major sports alliances use a similar regular season schedule after the end of the regular season. In addition to major league level organizations, there are also a few small sports and professional alliances that are active in smaller cities throughout the country. As in Canada and Australia, the United States Sports League does not carry out promotion and demotion, which is different from many sports consortium in Europe.

In the United States, sports are particularly related to education, and most high schools and universities have organized sports activities. College sports competition plays an important role in American sports culture. College basketball and college football are also popular in some parts of the United States. The main sanctioning institution for college sports is the National Collegiate Athletic Association (NCAA). Unlike most other countries, the United States government does not provide funds for sports nor for the United States Olympic Committee.

Automobile Culture

After the Second World War, people's dependence on cars grew rapidly, reinventing life in the cities and suburbs of the United States. It creates the suburban landscape and culture of contemporary American life. Having a car makes it easier for the white middle class and the working class family to move to the vast suburbs. Local and national transportation policies often encourage suburbanization, which was disadvantageous to old cities.

By the 1950s, more and more serious traffic problems and rapid suburbanization have threatened the future of the central business district of Chicago. In response, the city government has implemented a series of traffic projects aimed at encouraging the development of the city center. On the contrary, "improvement" encourages people and enterprises to move out of the city. Park Forest is one of the suburbs attracting Chicago residents, a planned development where the landscape and the rhythm of daily life revolved around the family car.

Since the 1950s, American car culture has had a lasting impact on American culture, mainly reflected in popular music. At the end of World War II, the manufacturing economy in the United States changed from production related products to consumer products. By the end of the 1950s, 1/6 of American workers were directly or interactively employed in the automotive industry. The United States has become the world's largest car manufacturer. 30 years ago, Henry Ford's goal—anyone who has good jobs should be able to afford a car—has already been realized.

The National Association for Stock Car Auto Racing (NASCAR) is the second most popular spectator sport in the United States, second only to the National Football League (NFL). It was merged by Bill Frances on 21, 1948, and took root in the 1950s. In 1952, the first "super highway asphalt", Darington Expressway, was opened in South Carolina, and the movement had a tremendous growth in the 1950s. Due to the great success in Darlington, a 2. 5

mile high embankment superspeedway began in the vicinity of the Daytona Beach, which is still in use.

As more and more Americans start driving cars, new business categories come into being, enabling them to enjoy their products and services without leaving their cars. This includes the drive-in restaurant, and the later drive-through window. Even in 2010, the Sonic Drive-in chain also provided 3,561 restaurants in the U. S. , serving 3 million customers a day. The company is famous for using roller skating shoes and holds a competition every year to determine the top roller skates in its system.

The drive-in theater is a cinema structure, including a large outdoor screen, a projection booth, a concession stand and a large parking area, where customers are watching movies from the comfort of a car, and listen by an electrodynamics loudspeaker placed in each parking space.

Part II   *High School Musical*

High School Musical is a 2006 American musical film, and the first part of the *High School Musical* trilogy was directed by Kenny Ortega. It was filmed in 2005 in Salt Lake City and was released on 20 July 2006, becoming the most successful film of the Disney Channel Original Movie (DCOM). The sequel of the movie "*High School Musical 2*" was released in 2007, and the feature film "*High School Musical 3*" was released in October 2008. It's the first and only DCOM to have a drama sequel, the film's soundtrack is the top-selling album in the United States in 2006.

Part Ⅲ   Listening and Speaking Activities

Task 1: Watch and listen to the Clip: *Can I Have This Dance.*
Fill in the following blanks with the exact words or phrases you hear.

Can I Have This Dance

［Gabriella］

Take my hand, _____

Pull me close and take one step

_____ on mine

And let the music _____

［Troy, Gabriella］

Won't you _____（now won't you promise me, that
you'll never forget）

We'll keep dancing（to keep dancing）wherever we go next

［Chorus］

It's like _____ the chances of finding someone like you

It's one in a million

the chances of feeling the way we do

And with _____

we just _____

So can I have this dance（can I have this dance）

Can I have this dance

[Troy]

Take my hand, I'll take the _____

And every turn will be _____ with me

Don't be afraid, afraid to fall

You know I'll catch you through it all

[Troy, Gabriella]

And you can't _____ (even a thousand miles, can't

keep us apart)

'Cause my heart is (cause my heart is) wherever you are

[Chorus]

It's like catching lightning the chances of finding someone like you

It's one in a million

the chances of feeling the way we do

And with every step together

we just keep on getting better

So can I have this dance (can I have this dance)

Can I have this dance

[Gabriella And Troy]

Oh no _____ too high enough, _____

too wide

'Cause together or not, our dance won't stop

Let it rain, let it pour

What we have is worth _____

You know I believe, that we were meant to be

[Chorus]

It's like catching lightning

the chances of finding someone like you (like you)

It's one in a million

the chances of feeling the way we do (way we do)

And with every step together

we just keep on getting better

So can I have this dance (can I have this dance)

Task 2: Read aloud the following lyrics, then watch the Clip:
Right Here, Right Now and sing after the singers.

Right Here, Right Now

Can you imagine, what would happen

if we could have any dream

I'd wish this moment, was ours to own it

and that it would never leave.

Then I would thank that star,

that made our wish come true (come true)

Oh Yeah

Cause he knows that where you are, is where I should be too.

[Chorus]

Right Here, Right Now

I'm looking at you, and my heart loves the view

'Cause you mean everything

Right Here, I promise you somehow

that tomorrow can wait, some other day to be (to be)

But right now there's you and me

[Vanessa]

It feels like forever, what could be better

We've already proved it was

That two thousand words, twenty three hours, have blended the universe.

Its gonna be, everything (everything)

in our whole world changed

(it starts changing)

and do know that when we are, (when we are)

our memory's the same

oh no, oh no

[Chorus]

Right Here, Right Now (right now)

I'm looking at you, and my heart loves the view

'Cause you mean everything (everything)

Right Here, I promise you somehow (somehow were gonna)

That tomorrow can wait, some other day to be (to be)

But right now there's you and me.

[Bridge]

Oh we know its coming (coming)

Oh its coming fast

It's always you and me, oh yeah

so lets make this second last

make it last

[Chorus]

Right here,

Ooohh Right now.

Yeah I'm looking at you,

and my heart loves the view

'Cause you mean everything

Right Here, I promise you somehow

That tomorrow can wait, some other day to be (to be)

But right now there's you and me

You and me

you and me

Oh You and me

But right now there's you and me

Task 3: Watch and listen to the Clip: *Just Getting Started.*
Answer the following questions.

1. What is the song "Just Getting started" mainly about? Find
out the words and expressions to illustrate your point.

_____

2. Try to describe the feelings in this song. The following
vocabulary and expressions are for your reference.

hopeful	promising	be high in spirits	cant bear to part with
fearless	idealistic	move on the more wit	in great delights
cheerful	elated	bright prospects	jubilant

Task 4: Watch the Clip: *Troy Bolton's Graduation Speech*. Answer the following questions.

1. Describe Troy's feeling at that moment.

2. Suppose you are elected to give a speech upon graduation from senior high school. Make a speech to tell the audience about your feeling, your hope, your promise etc.

Task 5: Reflect on memorable sentences. There are twelve songs in *High School Musical 3: Senior Year*, and which lyrics are still in your mind? Work in groups and tell each other your understanding of the following famous remarks.

1. This is the last time to get it right.

2. Now or never.

3. Right Here, Right Now

4. Just trust your heart. To find what you're here for, open another door.

5. We're all in this together.

6. Fight to find myself, me and no one else!

7. Life is coming, and I can't wait.

8. See you later doesn't mean goodbye.

9. Every memory of the sweet sunshine is living here in my heart.

10. You know a friend becomes a part of you, like this dream is finally coming true.

11. No goodbyes, because eyes can't bear to say it.

12. If my heart breaks, it's gonna hurt so bad.

Part IV   Movie Review and Projects

The High School Musical Series

David Nusair

That *High School Musical* has been crafted to appeal solely to young girls is obvious almost immediately, and while it seems fairly clear that they'll thrill to the antics of the film's broad characters, there's really not a whole lot here to hold the interest of most other viewers. True to its title, the movie is a flat-out musical set within the halls of a typical American high school—albeit one where students often **spontaneously** break out into song. The story revolves around jock Troy and brain Gabriella, both of whom have an obvious penchant for singing but are afraid to audition for the school musical for fear of alienating their friends (ie: Troy's basketball teammates). Director Kenny Ortega apes the look and feel of an old-fashioned musical, infusing the film with a distinctly larger-than-life vibe— something that's particularly true of the manner in which the characters relate to each other (think Grease, except with far less interesting actors). And although the movie is mindlessly engaging for a while, the whole thing ultimately becomes so overwhelmingly silly and juvenile; it's difficult to imagine even the most die-hard fan of musicals finding anything here worth embracing.

Though undoubtedly a marginal improvement over its thoroughly mediocre **predecessor**, *High School Musical 2* nevertheless possesses few elements designed to capture (and hold) viewers over a certain age. This is despite an **affable** opening half hour that's surprisingly engaging, as the central characters—including Zac Efron's Troy, Vanessa Hudgens'Gabriella, and Ashley Tisdale's Sharpay—celebrate the end of the school year with a series of increasingly energetic musical numbers. It's only as the action shifts to the country club where Troy and company have decided to spend their summer that one's interest slowly-but-surely starts to wane, with the inclusion of several eye-rollingly hoary plot developments proving **instrumental** in the film's ultimate downfall.

This is especially true of the whole Sharpay-engineers-Troy's-ascent-within-the-club subplot, as it invariably triggers a number of woefully melodramatic interludes and confrontations (ie: Troy's success effectively alienates him from his friends and leads to a fake break-up with Gabriella). And while it does go without saying that young girls will find plenty here worth embracing, *High School Musical 2's* relentlessly superficial supermodel ensures that it (and its forebearer) hardly reflects the best that the musical genre has to offer.

Though clearly the most cinematic of the series, *High School Musical 3: Senior Year* suffers from precisely the same sort of problems that plagued its two underwhelming predecessors with the trite storyline and hopelessly overlong running time ranking at the top of the film's list of deficiencies. True to its title, the movie follows the various students at East High as they prepare for their impending graduation and revolves primarily around Troy (Zac Efron) and Gabriella's (Vanessa Hudgens) indecision regarding their respective futures. Director Kenny Ortega—working from Peter Barsocchini's screenplay—has infused the majority of the movie's musical sequences with a distinctly stagy sensibility that ultimately proves oppressive, as there's simply no overlooking the filmed-play atmosphere that comes to dominate the opening hour. And while there are a few exceptions to this—ie a surprisingly dark number in which Troy angrily weighs his options—*High School Musical 3*: *Senior Year* is primarily dominated by interludes that seem to have emerged directly from a theatrical staging of the material. The relentlessly superficial atmosphere only exacerbates the movie's various problems, with the affable work of the various performers— Efron is especially good here-slowly-but-surely rendered moot by the egregious emphasis on lightheartedness. To be fair, Barsocchini does inject the proceedings with desperately-needed instances of depth towards the almost **melancholic** conclusion, yet this hardly proves effective enough to lift the movie out of its unmistakable **doldrums**. The end result is a trilogy capper that matches its predecessors in terms of quality, thus ensuring that *High School Musical* fans will find as much here to embrace as detractors will find to dislike.

The *High School Musical* series returns to its small screen origins with *Sharpay's Fabulous Adventure*, which follows periphery character Sharpay Evans (Ashley Tisdale) as she leaves her hometown of Albuquerque for the bright lights of New York City-where she hopes to make it as an actress on Broadway. Upon arriving at her first audition, however, Sharpay is horrified to discover that the producers are more interested in her dog, Boi, than her—which effectively forces the character to hang around in the hopes that her adorable pup will eventually get the role. (There's also a subplot revolving around Sharpay's tentative romance with a scrappy local, Austin Butler's Peyton Leverett.) There's little doubt that *Sharpay's Fabulous Adventure* gets off to a nigh disastrous start, as director Michael Lembeck, working from Robert Horn's script, opens the proceedings with a bland and surprisingly low-rent musical number that immediately establishes an underwhelming atmosphere. The movie subsequently segues into a familiar story of a small town girl attempting to conquer the big city, which would be fine if Lembeck and Horn hadn't bogged the narrative down with elements of a decidedly (and eye-rollingly) adolescent variety—with the dumbed down vibe exacerbated by Horn's tendency to hit every single note that one might have anticipated (eg. Sharpay discovers that her hero is a jerk, Sharpay learns that friendship is more important than success, etc.). By the time the almost unreasonably upbeat finale rolls around, Sharpay's Fabulous Adventure has definitively established itself as a bottom-of-the-barrel endeavor that's destined to test the patience of even the hardiest of *High School Musical* fans. ❶

New Words and Phrases：

spontaneously	adv.	自然地,自发地,不由自主地; 不禁;油然
doldrums	n.	忧郁,无生气
affable	adj.	友善的,和蔼的
predecessor	n.	前任,前辈;原有事物,前身
instrumental	adj.	有帮助的,起作用的
melancholic	n.	忧郁症患者

Project 1：Work in groups and tell each other the reasons you like *High School Musical 3*.

Name	Reasons

---

❶ 1. David Nusair. The High School Musical Series [EB/OL]. 2006 [2018 – 03 – 05]. http://www. reelfilm. com/highmus. htm#1.

Project 2: Try to analyze the mechanics of the movie *High School Musical 3* and ask yourself what impression the movie left you in these areas:

1. Direction. Consider how the director chooses to describe the events in the story. If you have seen other movies directed by the same person, compare them and determine which one you like best.

2. Soundtrack. Does it work with the scene? A soundtrack can make or destroy a movie, especially when the song has specific information or meaning to them.

3. Clothing design. Does the choice of clothing conform to the style of the film? Do they help to create the overall tone, rather than deviate from it?

4. Setting design. Consider how the movie settings affect other elements. If the film was taken in a real place, is this location carefully selected?

5. Film photography. What techniques are used in the film? What background elements help to create a kind of tone?

Chapter X　Conflicts and Integration

Introduction to the Chapter

E pluribus unum, Latin for "Out of many, one," is a 13-letter traditional motto of the United States, appearing on the Great Seal as well as many American coins. Though the meaning of the phrase dates back to the concept that out of the union of the original thirteen colonies emerged a new single nation, it has been later interpreted as the "melting pot" ethos: blending diverse peoples into one through assimilation and integration. America has survived and thrived partly because of various ethnic groups of immigrants who have enriched America with diverse art, food, music, and literature while accepting a common culture of American values and institutions.

Part I　Cultural Foods

The Melting Pot

Traditionally called a melting pot, the United States has welcomed waves and waves of immigrants, who, with time,

have melted together, shedding the characteristics of their old cultures to become part of a new and uniquely American culture.

This "melting pot" metaphor, first arising in the eighteenth century, described the fusion of various religions, nationalities, and ethnic groups into one distinct people. It gained widespread popularity in the United States during the great wave of Slavic, Jewish, and Italian immigration in the 1900s, when an immigrant named Israel Zangwill produced a famous play, *The Melting Pot*, in which a character says with enthusiasm, "America is God's crucible, the great melting-pot where all the races of Europe are melting and re-forming!"

However, this process of melting, or in other words assimilation, entailed costs and sacrifice. Upon arriving in the United States, immigrants of diverse backgrounds were required to become American, learning the language, history, political principles, and customs that identified one as an American. This requirement was necessarily in conflict with their old cultures and values, and, eventually, resulted in a painful loss of old traditions and customs.

The American civil rights movement of the last half of the twentieth century aroused in people across the United States a new awareness of and pride in their ethnic origins. This multi-cultural consciousness triggered some to advocate abandoning the metaphor of a melting pot, and instead adopting another term, a salad bowl.

The Salad Bowl

Starting in the 1960s, the metaphor of the salad bowl, another vision of American pluralism, arose. Rather than assimilating, immigrants of diverse backgrounds now would coexist, keeping their unique identities just like the ingredients in a salad, bound

together instead of melted together. This observation reveals the ideology of multiculturalism, which far surpasses the demand that ethnic differences should be accepted rather than disparaged.

The notion of the United States as a salad bowl seems to have been popularized by the eminent historian Carl Degler. In his book *Out of Our Past: The Forces that Shaped Modern America*, he wrote: "some habits from the old country were not discarded; in those instances the children of immigrants even into the third and fourth generations retained their differences. In view of such failure to melt and fuse, the metaphor of the melting pot is unfortunate and misleading. A more accurate analogy would be a salad bowl, for, although the salad is an entity, the lettuce can still be distinguished from the chicory, the tomatoes from the cabbage."

Multiculturalism refers to the view that different cultures, races, and ethnicities, particularly those of minority groups, deserve special recognition of contributions to the cultural life of a dominant political culture. Such a notion is both a response to the fact of cultural pluralism in modern democracies and a way of compensating ethnic minorities for past exclusion, discrimination, and oppression. It seeks the inclusion of the views and contributions of diverse members of society while maintaining respect for their differences and withholding the demand for their assimilation into the dominant culture.

Since the 1960s, the American government has admitted, encouraged and supported multiculturalism: fair policies have endowed all citizens with the right to preserve their cultural inheritance; public school has launched bilingual education programs for new immigrants; new laws have significantly reduced racism, discrimination and prejudice against minorities. People of multicultural background are easy to accept different views, values and behaviors of foreign countries. Particularly, following the fast development of the Internet and wireless communication technology, the distance among countries or people has become closer, and the economies between regions and countries are connected more closely. The whole world became a global village. Multiculturalism is becoming more important than at any other time in history.

Part II   *Crash*

Crash, a 2004 American drama film produced, directed, and co-written by Paul Haggis, features the physical and emotional **collision** of a group of strangers in Los Angeles because of issues of race and gender.

Graham is a police detective with a street criminal brother, and it hurts him to know his mother cares more about his never-do-well brother than him. Graham's partner is Ria, also his girlfriend, though she has begun to **bristle** at his emotional distance, as well as his occasional **insensitivity** over the fact he's African-American and she's Hispanic.

Rick is an L. A. district attorney whose wife, Jean, makes little secret of her fear and hatred of people unlike herself. Jean's worst imaginings about people of color are confirmed when her SUV is carjacked by two African-American men: Anthony, who dislikes white people as much as Jean hates blacks, and Peter, who is more open-minded.

Cameron is a wealthy African-American television producer with a beautiful wife, Christine. While coming home from a party, Cameron and Christine are pulled over by Officer Ryan, who subjects them to a **humiliating interrogation** (and her to an inappropriate search) while his new partner, Officer Hansen, looks on.

Daniel is a hard-working locksmith and dedicated father who discovers that his looks don't lead many of his customers to trust him.

Farhad is a Middle Eastern shopkeeper who is so constantly threatened in the wake of the "9 · 11" attacks that he decides he needs a gun to defend his family.

New Words and Phrases:

collision	n.	抵触;碰撞(或相撞)事故
bristle	v.	大为恼怒;被激怒
insensitivity	n.	钝感;不灵敏度;不敏感性
humiliating	adj.	羞辱性的;丢脸的;耻辱的
interrogation	n.	审问;审讯;询问

Part III   Listening and Speaking Activities

Task 1: View and listen to the following clip: *Crash* and fill in the blanks with the missing words and expressions.

There is a crash at the beginning of the movie. It happens in
_____. The male in the car describes the crash as
_____ because they are always behind the
_____ and miss _____ so much that they
_____ to feel something. The female in the car thinks
they've got _____ and decides to go look for the
reason. When the policeman asks to see the _____
of the Asian woman, she insists that it's the white woman's
_____. The Asian woman blames the white woman for
_____ and stopping in the middle of the street. The
white woman is _____ to be hit by an Asian driver. At
the same time the policeman tries to make them _____.

New Words and Phrases:

bump into	v. phr.	碰撞
rear-end	v.	追尾
frame of reference	n. phr.	参照标准
steering wheel	n. phr.	方向盘
brake	v.	刹车

Task 2: View and listen to the following clip: *Two Black Guys Robbing a Car* and answer the following questions.

1. What does the conversation between the two black guys reflect?

_____

2. Are the two black guys intended to rob the car at the very beginning?

_____

3. Does the white woman discriminate against them as soon as she sees the two black guys?

_____

4. Why do the two black guys rob the car of the white couple?

_____

New Words and Phrases

spaghetti	n.	意大利面
stereotype	n.	陈规；刻板印象
size sb. up	v. phr.	估计，打量
tip	v & n.	（给）小费
battery	n.	电池
as a matter of fact	prep. phr.	实际上
stroll	v.	漫步；闲逛
gangbanger	n.	青少年犯罪团伙成员
over-caffeinated	adj.	含过量咖啡因的
patrol	v.	巡逻

trigger	n.	扳机

Task 3: View and listen to the following clip: *Cameron in Studio*, and decide whether each of the following statements is true or false.

1. Cameron is a black television director in the movie.

2. Jamal is a white coach in the program.

3. Fred is talking Cameron into doing it one more time.

4. "Don't talk to me about that" is a typical expression for the black.

New Words and Phrases:

scene	n.	场景
weird	adj.	怪异的；不可思议的

Task 4: View and listen to the following clip: *Ryan's Saving the Lady* and Discuss in a Group.

Jack Ryan is a Los Angeles Police Department (LAPD) officer, a 17 year veteran of the force. When he pulls over a black film director and his wife in a routine traffic stop and then harasses and fondles the woman, the woman is filled with hatred towards him. Here in this segment, Ryan risks his life to save the woman from the fire caused by a traffic accident even when the woman at first insists that he keep away from her. What do you think of Ryan? What kind of person is he? What does this episode have to do with the theme of the movie?

Useful Words and Expressions for Your Reference:

dignity	interrelate	complicated	gender and race	human nature
enrage	intertwine	discrimination	human collision	dual character
evoke	immigrants	preconception	thought – provoking	two – dimensional
arouse	confront	stereotype	be confronted with	multiple characters
racism	prejudice	justice	on the basis of class	

New Words and Phrases:

paramedic	n.	护理人员；急救人员
extinguisher	n.	灭火器
filthy	adj.	肮脏的；污秽的
lap	n.	大腿

Task 5：View and listen to the following clip：*Clash between a Mexican Locksmith and a Persian Storeowner* and work in groups of four and role play this segment, playing the role of the locksmith, the storeowner, the daughter and the mommy respectively. You may refer to the script.

New Words and Phrases:

bro	n.	兄弟(brother 的简称)
call sb. names	v. phr.	骂某人
impenetrable	adj.	不能穿透的；刀枪不入的
cloak	n.	斗篷；披风

Task 6：Reflect on memorable sentences. Which sentences are still in your mind? Which sentence impresses you most? Why? Share

your understanding of the sentences with your friends. Some sentences are listed below for your reference.

1. It's the sense of touch. In any real city, you walk, you know? You brush past people, people bump into you. In L. A. , nobody touches you. We're always behind this metal and glass. I think we miss that touch so much, that we crash into each other, just so we can feel something.

2. She had these little stubby wings, like she could've glued them on, you know, like I'm gonna believe she's a fairy. So she said, "I'll prove it. " So she reaches into her backpack and she pulls out this invisible cloak and she ties it around my neck. And she tells me that it's impenetrable. You know what impenetrable means? It means nothing can go through it. No bullets, nothing. She told me that if I wore it, nothing would hurt me. So I did. And my whole life, I never got shot, stabbed, nothing. I mean, how weird is that?

Part IV   Movie Review and Projects

A Movie Review of *Crash*

James Berardinelli

Ensemble features can be daunting, yet some filmmakers embrace the challenge, and their results reward an audience. A lot of characters are woven into the **tapestry** of *Crash*, the feature directing debut of TV veteran Paul Haggis. (Haggis was also Oscar nominated for writing the screenplay of *Million Dollar Baby*.) The story unfolds in Los Angeles, where **hostility** is often a barrier to intimacy, and hatred and fear cloud judgment. Don Cheadle plays Graham Waters, a police detective investigating what may be a racially-motivated killing. Graham is having an affair with his Latina partner (Jennifer Esposito), whom he variously refers to as "a white woman" and "Mexican," neither of which is accurate. Matt Dillon is LAPD officer Jack Ryan, a 17 year veteran of the force whose actions often cross the line. When he fondles a woman (Thandie Newton) during a routine traffic stop, his partner (Ryan Phillippe) wants to sever their professional relationship. Meanwhile, the D. A. , Rick Cameron (Brendan Fraser), and his wife, Jean (Sandra Bullock), become crime victims when their car is stolen by a pair of thieves

(Chris "Ludicris" Bridges and Larenz Tate).

The best ensemble films are the ones in which the characters are given an opportunity to breathe (Magnolia, Short Cuts, and Nashville come to mind). With *Crash*, 105 minutes is barely enough time to let the numerous participants begin to inhale. The movie runs for long enough to allow Haggis to present the story, but we're left wanting a little more—a few extra scenes and an added conversation or two (especially between Newton's character and her husband, played by Terrence Dashon Howard). But I suppose it's always best to leave an audience hungry, rather than feeling **overstuffed**.

Crash's strength is that it deals intelligently with serious subjects. Racism is a hot-button issue, yet Haggis manages to approach it in a universal, reasonable manner. We don't feel like we're being preached to, nor does this seem like a **sanctimonious** "message movie". The film's numerous stories are tied together by a web of coincidence. Af first, there's a sense that so much contrivance invites criticism. However, on a second viewing, I was aware of the balance and symmetry in the way the characters' tales connect, sometimes only **tangentially**. Haggis has created a microcosmos, so it's only right for plot-lines to criss-cross.

The director has assembled a large, accomplished cast that includes Matt Dillon, Don Cheadle, Sandra Bullock, Thandie Newton, and Ryan Phillippe. Amongst other things, this group virtually assures that the film will be seen. All are more than competent in their roles—with Cheadle, Dillon, and Newton being especially memorable—and each does his or her best to enhance the two-dimensionality of the characters as they are presented in the screenplay. The most powerful scene in *Crash* has Dillon and Newton confronting mistrust on the cusp of mortality.

The principle subject matter is racism and its **manifestations**, and how it is often as much the result of social conditioning and anger as of hatred and intolerance. In addition to the usual white-on-black manifestation of discrimination, we are confronted with black-on-Latino, Latino-on-Asian, white-on-Middle Eastern, and other permutations. Wherever cultural differences exist, there is room for tension. However, by depicting **bigoted** characters as otherwise caring individuals, *Crash* asks us to consider the causes of racism as much as to examine its effects. In doing this, *Crash* sets itself apart, at least to a degree, from other, similar motion pictures. Although an expanded running time would have afforded us the opportunity to get to know the characters better, *Crash* is long enough to permit the film's themes to strike a responsive chord. ❶

New Words and Phrases:

ensemble	n.	整体;全体;全套服装
tapestry	n.	挂毯;织锦;壁毯;绣帷
hostility	n.	敌意;对抗

---

❶ 1. James Berardinelli. Crash [EB/OL]. [2016 – 12 – 24]. http://www. reelviews. net/php_review_template. php? identifier = 156.

overstuffed	adj.	填塞很多的;涂油过多的;多油的
sanctimonious	adj.	装作圣洁的;伪善的;道貌岸然的
tangentially	adv.	无关地
manifestation	n.	显示;表示;表明
bigoted	adj.	顽固盲从的;偏执的

Project 1: Search information on the Internet about culture shock and answer the following questions in a group.

1. What is culture shock?

_____

2. What stages does culture shock consist of?

_____

_____

_____

_____

3. How can we adapt to a new environment quickly?

_____

_____

_____

_____

Project 2: Suppose some foreign friends want to know something about traditional Chinese festivals. Choose at least two from the following list and introduce them to your friends. You may first fill in the table.

1. Spring Festival

2. Lantern Festival

3. Qingming Day

4. Dragon Boat Festival

5. Double Seventh Festival

6. Mid-Autumn Festival

7. Double Ninth Festival

_____ Festival	
Date	
Places	
History	
Customs	

References

[1] American Work Ethic [EB/OL]. (2013 − 05 − 04) [2016 − 09 − 10]. http://www. ronperrier. net/2013/05/04/american − work − ethic.

[2] Art Swift. American's Trust in Mass Media Sinks to New Low. [EB/OL]. (2016 − 09 − 14) [2017 − 03 − 11]. http://www. gallup. com/poll/195542.

[3] Ashley Dugger. Development of the Mass Media and Journalism in the United States [EB/OL]. [2018 − 03 − 15]. http://study. com/academy/lesson.

[4] C Verlag. Inventing The Modern American Family [EB/OL]. 2013 [2017 − 09 − 08]. https://academic. oup. com/jah/article/100/3/883/762769.

[5] Crash [EB/OL]. (2008 − 07 − 19) [2018 − 02 − 12]. https://www. rottentomatoes. com/m/1144992_crash.

[6] David Nusair. The High School Musical Series [EB/OL]. [2018 − 03 − 05]. http://www. reelfilm. com/highmus. htm#1.

[7] Family Life, 20th − Century Families [EB/OL]. [2017 − 09 − 15]. http://www. countriesquest. com/north_america/usa/people.

[8] James Berardinelli. Crash [EB/OL]. [2016 − 12 − 24]. http://www. reelviews. net/php_review_template. php? identifier = 156.

[9] Mass Media and Its Influence on American Culture [EB/OL]. (2013 − 05 − 20) [2018 − 02 − 21]. https://makaylaheisler. wordpress. com.

[10] Media of United States [EB/OL]. [2017 − 03 − 25]. https://en.

wikipedia. org/wiki.

[11]Nina Katungi. American Beauty 1000 Movie Review [EB/OL]. [2017 –
11 – 11]. http://www. wildsound – filmmaking – feedback – events. com.

[12]Religion and Public Life [EB/OL]. (2015 – 08 – 27) [2017 – 06 – 01].
http://www. pewforum. org.

[13]Religion in the United States [EB/OL]. (2001 – 12 – 19) [2017 – 05 –
15]. https://en. wikipedia. org/wiki.

[14]Roger Ebert. The Devil Wears Prada [EB/OL]. (2006 – 06 – 29) [2016 –
12 – 12]. https://www. rogerebert. com/reviews/ the – devil – wears –
prada – 2006.

[15]Roger Ebert. The Shawshank Redemption [EB/OL]. (1994 – 09 – 23)
[2016 – 11 – 05]. https://www. rogerebert. com/reviews.

[16]Roger Elbert. A Controlled World [EB/OL]. (1998 – 06 – 05) [2017 –
11 – 15]. https://www. rogerebert. com/reviews.

[17]Stacy Taylor. American Family Values [EB/OL]. [2017 – 01 – 14].
http://family. lovetoknow. com/american – family – values.

[18] Stephen Hunter. Saving Private Ryan [EB/OL]. (1998 – 07 – 24)
[2018 – 02 – 03]. http://www. washingtonpost. com/wp – srv/style/
longterm/movies.

[19] 10 Facts about Religion in America [EB/OL]. [2017 – 04 – 12].
http://www. pewresearch. org/fact – tank.

[20]The Evolution of the Mass Media [EB/OL]. [2018 – 03 – 06]. https://
www. cliffsnotes. com/study – guides/sociology.

[21]The Meaning of Truman Show [EB/OL]. [2017 – 04 – 22]. http://
www. transparencynow. com/trusig. htm.

[22]The Pursuit of Happiness [EB/OL]. [2017 – 04 – 22]. https://www.

pluggedin. com/movie – reviews.

[23] The Ten Commandments [EB/OL]. (2014 – 07 – 12) [2017 – 12 – 05]. https://www. hollywoodreporter. com/news.

[24] Tricia Hussung. The Evolution of American Family Structure [EB/OL]. (2015 – 06 – 23) [2016 – 12 – 13]. http://online. csp. edu/blog/family – science.

[25] Understanding the American Education System [EB/OL]. (2017 – 06 – 12) [2017 – 12 – 05]. https://www. studyusa. com/en/a/58.

[26] Vincent Canby. The Dead Poet Society [EB/OL]. [2017 – 12 – 05]. http://movies. nytimes. com/movie/review.